North Carolina

OUR STATE GOVERNMENT

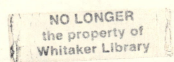

North Carolina Capitol—Raleigh

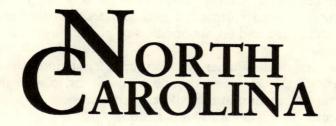

NORTH CAROLINA

OUR STATE GOVERNMENT

1983

LUCILLE HOWARD

THE LEAGUE OF WOMEN VOTERS OF NORTH CAROLINA

Published by Carolina Academic Press
Durham, North Carolina

The League of Women Voters is recognized and valued for its efforts to encourage voter registration and voting.

The League of Women Voters leads the way in providing solid non-partisan information on candidates and ballot issues at election time and on major issues of public concern at all times.

The League of Women Voters shapes legislation at every governmental level to meet the public's needs and to strengthen citizen participation in the political process.

Membership is open to all persons.

Printed in the United States of America

Carolina Academic Press
PO Box 8795, Forest Hills Station
Durham, North Carolina 27707

TABLE OF CONTENTS

Brinegar Cabin—Blue Ridge Parkway

LIST OF MAPS, CHARTS AND ILLUSTRATIONS

ACKNOWLEDGMENTS

The following business and civic leaders have made this book possible by contributing generously to the League of Women Voters of North Carolina and the League of Women Voters Education Fund.

James C. and Diane D. Brown

Broyhill Foundation, Inc.

Burlington Industries Foundation

Burroughs Wellcome Co.

Celanese/Fiber Industries, Inc.

Ciba-Geigy Corporation

Elizabeth Wade Grant

International Business Machines Corporation

Lowe's Companies, Inc.

Jarmila McMullen

Nationwide Mutual Insurance Company

Olsen Associates, Inc., Engineers and Architects

R. J. Reynolds Tobacco Company, an operating company of R. J. Reynolds Industries, Inc.

Rose's Stores, Inc.

Adele M. Thomas Trust

Winn-Dixie Raleigh, Inc.

NOTES

Students of state government will find that its organization changes frequently as new agencies are opened, as new advisory boards are created, as old commissions are abolished. Election laws, also, are subject to frequent changes.

As this book is printed, a joint legislative committee on the separation of powers is studying and proposing changes in the relationship between the legislative and executive branches of government. Recent rulings that the legislature has inserted itself inappropriately in executive functions may result in some changes in state government. For example, it is expected the legislature will soon vote to remove legislators from membership on more than 44 of the governor's boards and commissions.

Redistricting maps for the U.S. Congress and N. C. House and Senate have been approved by the N.C. General Assembly and the U.S. Department of Justice, but are being challenged in court at this writing.

Election laws, as well as names of boards and commissions, are subject to frequent changes.

Occasional (G.S.) notations refer to the General Statute(s) where additional information may be found regarding a topic.

The author wishes to acknowledge the valuable assistance of many persons who gave time and thought to the publication of this book.

Suggestions and critical reading by Ann Sawyer and Dr. Milton Heath, Jr., of the Institute of Government, and John L. Cheney, Jr., director of publications and editor of the *North Carolina Manual* for the Office of the Secretary of State, were particularly valuable. Elected and appointed officials of the state government and staff were very generous in providing materials and suggestions.

League members who provided special information were Helen Pratt, Camille McGeachy and Cynthia Wertz. University of North Carolina at Charlotte professors Dr. Ed Perzel and Dr. Bill McCoy, N.C. Representative Louise Brennan, and Marvin Dorman and Leslie Bevacqua, both in the Office of the Governor, provided helpful information, as did many others.

LWVNC Presidents Diane Brown and Marion Nichol and members of the state board have made this book possible through their encouragement, direction and support. Funding the project was the special assignment of Claudia Kadis. League members who read the manuscript and offered guidance were Diane Brown, Helen Pratt and Ellen Olson.

Foundation for the book was established by Wilma R. Davidson, editor of the 1976 edition. Two previous editions, in 1969, edited by Sylvia Ruby, and in 1954 (editor unknown), also had been printed.

George Breisacher is the Charlotte artist whose work illustrates this book.

Most organizational charts are from the *North Carolina Manual*.

—Lucille Howard

QUICK FACTS ABOUT NORTH CAROLINA

Population (1980 Census): 5,881,813, includes 4,457,507 Whites, 1,318,857 Blacks, 64,652 American Indians, 21,176 Asians, and 19,574 of other races.

Statehood: 1789, twelfth state to enter the union.

Capital: Raleigh

Counties: 100, the final division made in 1911.

Area: 52,712 sq. miles.

Highest elevation: Mt. Mitchell, 6,684 ft.

State bird: cardinal

NORTH CAROLINA: OUR STATE GOVERNMENT

State flower: dogwood

State insect: honey bee

State tree: pine

State mammal: gray squirrel

State shell: Scotch bonnet

State salt water fish: channel bass (red drum)

State reptile: turtle

State rock: granite

State precious stone: emerald

State colors: red and blue

Motto: Esse Quam Videri (To be rather than to seem).

Name: Carolina is from the word Carolus, the Latin form of Charles. King Charles I of England chose the name.

Nicknames: "Old North State," applied to the older, northern settlement when Carolina was divided in 1710.

"Tarheel State," applied after a battle in the Civil War when a N.C. regiment was kidded about tar being one of the state's principal products. The N.C. soldiers, who had won the battle on their own, said next time they would put tar on the heels of the other soldiers to make them stick better in the next fight. On hearing this, Gen. Lee is said to have blessed the "Tar Heel boys."[1]

1. John L. Cheney, Jr. (Editor), *North Carolina Manual 1979* (Raleigh: Office of the Secretary of State, 1979), p. 37.

INTRODUCTION:

THE TARHEEL STATE TODAY

North Carolina stretches a distance of 503 miles from the eastern tip of Dare County on the Atlantic Ocean to the western tip of Cherokee County in the Great Smoky Mountains. The state is divided into three natural regions: the coastal plain, the piedmont and the Appalachian Mountain region.

The coastal area has been a traditional vacation region and is experiencing development in commercial fishing and as a port area. Inland, the eastern section remains primarily a settlement of small farms. The sparsely populated mountain region also is developing into a major tourist area with its winter sports, camping, natural resources and folk crafts. Industry is concentrated in the more populous piedmont, dominated by the state's largest city—Charlotte, the Triangle area—Raleigh, Durham, and Chapel Hill and the Triad area—Greensboro, High Point and Winston-Salem.

The climate of North Carolina is described as humid, subtropical and is characterized by short, mild winters and long, hot summers. The transitional seasons are very pleasant and beautiful with spring flowers and fall foliage. Most precipitation is in rain, averaging 50 inches per year, although there is some snowfall in the winter, particularly in the mountain area.

A dense network of rivers cuts across the state. Most of these drain to the Atlantic Ocean. Major rivers flowing east are the Roanoke, Tar-Pamlico, Neuse, Cape Fear, Lumber, Yadkin-Pee Dee, Catawba and the Broad. The New, Watauga, French Broad and Little Tennessee Rivers flow west toward the Ohio and Tennessee Rivers.

North Carolina's population was 5,881,813 after the 1980 U.S. Census, making it the tenth most populous state. Per capita personal income in 1979 ranged from a low of $3,677 in Hyde County to a high of $9,737 in Mecklenburg County, compared with a national average of $8,757.[1] Per capita taxes collected from North Carolinians were $712 ($521, state; $191, local) in 1978-79, compared to the national average of $935 ($569, state; $365, local) for that year.[2] State and local government expenditures per capita in 1977 were $928.08, compared to the national average of $1,261.96.[3]

Once known for its tar, pitch and turpentine, North Carolina now has a reputation for being the nation's leading producer of tobacco, wood furniture, textiles and brick products.

North Carolina leads the nation in production of tobacco and farm forest products. The state ranks eleventh in cash receipts from crops and thirteenth in all farm commodities. Other important agricultural products are sweet potatoes, broilers, hogs, soybeans, corn, dairy products, eggs, cattle, turkeys, peanuts, greenhouse and nursery products, apples and wheat. Some 34.8% of the state's land is used in farming.

Manufactured goods of North Carolina are led by textile mill products. The rest of the top ten products are tobacco products, food, chemicals and allied products, furniture and fixtures, electronics equipment, non-electric machinery, apparel, fabricated metal products and paper products. North Carolina ranks tenth in the number of manufacturing employees, with more than 800,000. Increased growth of the electronics industry is anticipated in the state with the creation of a microelectronics center in the Triangle area.

In 1959 the state established Research Triangle Park, a 5,400-acre tract in the Raleigh, Durham, Chapel Hill area. Home to some 30 major corporations and government agencies whose research facilities are located there, the park is situated to take advantage of the research capabilities at three close-by universities: UNC at Chapel Hill, N.C. State University and Duke University.

1. *North Carolina State Data Center*, Vol. 3, No. 2, (Raleigh: Office of State Budget and Management), April, 1981, p. 9.
2. *North Carolina: Tax Guide 1981*, (Raleigh: Office of State Budget and Management), 1981, p. 89.
3. "Factors Favorable to Industry in North Carolina," (Raleigh: N.C. Department of Commerce, Industrial Development Division).

Other important businesses in the state are finance, banking and insurance.

Tourists travel to North Carolina in increasing numbers each year to take advantage of year-round recreational opportunities. Residents and visitors alike crowd the beaches, play golf on more than 300 courses in the state, hike the Appalachian Trail, drive the Blue Ridge Parkway, ski in the mountains in winter or hang glide in summer, camp in four national forests or 19 sites in the state parks system and tour numerous historic attractions.

The state claims several firsts in the area of art and culture: the first state department devoted to cultural resources, the first state-funded symphony orchestra, the first state-purchased art collection, the first state-supported outdoor drama, the first state-established school for the performing arts and the first public residential high school for selected students gifted and talented in math and science.

Military training facilities located in North Carolina include Camp Lejeune, near Jacksonville, a Marine Corps amphibious training base and the south's largest Naval hospital. At Cherry Point, between New Bern and Morehead City, is the Marine Corps Air Station and the Naval Air Rework Facility. A U.S. Coast Guard station is located at Elizabeth City. Fort Bragg, one of the largest military installations in the United States, is near Fayetteville. Adjoining it is Pope Air Force Base, a part of the Tactical Air Command. Seymour Johnson Air Force Base, near Goldsboro, is also a Tactical Air Command installation.

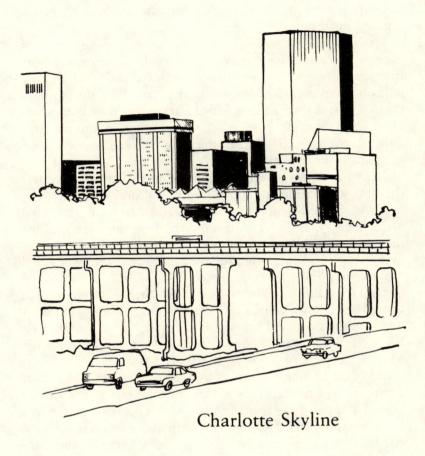

Charlotte Skyline

CHAPTER I.

GOVERNMENT IN THE HISTORY OF NORTH CAROLINA

The first recorded government in North Carolina was headed by the Lords Proprietors beginning in 1663. In that year, King Charles II of England granted a proprietary charter to eight British statesmen. That was nearly 130 years after the first explorations in the region by the Florentine Giovanni da Verrazzano and some 75 years after the first English attempts at settlement on Roanoke Island.

The date of the first permanent settlement in North Carolina is unknown, but the settlers moved south from the expanding Virginia colony into the Chowan River and Albermarle Sound area. The governor of Virginia and his council began to issue land grants along the Chowan River in 1662 and appointed a "commander of the southern plantation."[1] Settlement had spread to the Blue Ridge Mountains by the time of the Revolutionary War. The present boundaries of North Carolina were established in 1789.

The Lords Proprietors

King Charles' 1663 charter to the large territory called Carolina (amended two years later to include the Albemarle Sound settlements and lands even south of St. Augustine, in Florida[2]) superceded the Virginia land grants and was the

---

1. William S. Powell, *Ye County of Albemarle*, (Raleigh: North Carolina Department of Archives and History, 1958), p. xxiii.
2. Hugh T. Lefler and Albert R. Newsome, *North Carolina: The History of a Southern State* (3rd Ed.), (Chapel Hill: UNC Press, 1973), p. 35.

first extension of English colonization into the Spanish-claimed region.[3] The eight Lords Proprietors, who received the charter, appointed a governor and council, issued land grants, levied taxes and encouraged trade.

Control of the government rested with the governor and council, who exercised executive, legislative and judicial powers. Twelve elected representatives were included in a parliament with the appointed officials. It had no power to initiate legislation, however.[4] The governor and council also constituted the first court system, although it was later expanded to include appointed justices. The appointed sheriff was the primary governmental officer at the local level.

After a bicameral (two-house) legislative system was adopted in 1697, the council served as the upper house, and representatives elected by the people made up the lower house.[5] Each precinct (called a county after 1735) and certain towns had a representative. The assembly of elected representatives could meet only when called together by the governor. However, its limited powers included initiating money matters and setting the governor's salary, a constant source of controversy between the governor and lower house.[6]

In 1712 the Lords Proprietors divided Carolina into two distinct colonies. Edward Hyde was appointed the first governor of North Carolina.

A Royal Colony

In 1729 seven of the Lords Proprietors sold their interest in North Carolina to the crown, and the territory became a royal colony. The eighth proprietor retained the Carteret share which became known as the Granville district. There was no significant change in the structure of the government except that the king and the Privy Council appointed the governor and council and determined their powers and duties.

---

3. *Ibid.*, p. 32.
4. *Ibid.*, p. 46-47.
5. John L. Cheney, Jr. (Editor), *North Carolina Manual 1979*, (Raleigh: Office of the Secretary of State, 1979), p. 283.
6. *Ibid.*

There was a decided change, however, in the "spirit and efficiency of administration," as the crown emphasized the promotion of the naval stores industry (from the state's tar, pitch and turpentine) and other activities bringing about rapid growth in population.[7] The royal government also provided more stability with stronger administration and better law enforcement than had the proprietors.

The Revolutionary War

Protests against unfair taxes and other oppression by the proprietary government had led to the formation of a group called the Regulators. They were particularly concerned with justice for the residents of the counties in the western part of the colony and formed a military force which was defeated by the governor's militia in the Battle of Alamance in 1771.

The movement protesting injustice was interrupted by the coming of the American Revolution. Patriot activities forced the royal governor to flee in 1775, and the Provincial Congress took over control of government. Sessions were held in New Bern, Halifax and Hillsborough. The Halifax Resolves were adopted on April 12, 1776, and North Carolina became the first colony to sanction American independence. The year before, the Mecklenburg County Committee of Safety had adopted a set of "resolves" on May 31, 1775, declaring that all commissions granted by the King were "null and void" and urging the citizens to elect officers who would hold their powers "independent of Great Britain."[8] Some Mecklenburg residents recalled, however, that a meeting was held in Charlotte May 20, 1775, and a document was written declaring the citizens to be "free and independent people." The so-called Mecklenburg Declaration of Independence was written from memory in 1800 by John McNitt Alexander after his papers burned in a fire, and no newspaper accounts or other documents have ever been discovered to document its authenticity, according to UNCC history professor Dr. Edward

7. Lefler and Newsome, p. 77.
8. *Ibid.*, p. 205.

Perzel. Legislators added the signatures in 1831. The declaration remains a source of controversy, although its date, May 20, 1775, was added to the state flag in 1861 and to the state seal in 1893.

At the end of the Revolution, citizens of North Carolina rejected the federal Constitution in 1788. They did so because they feared a strong central government, a result of their experience with proprietary control, and because the document contained no guarantee of personal freedoms. The next year, however, another convention reversed that stand and ratified the Constitution even before the Bill of Rights was added.[9] North Carolina became the twelfth state to enter the Union.

The Constitution of 1776

North Carolina's first Constitution, adopted in 1776, outlined the state government and contained a Declaration of Rights which secured the rights of the citizen from interference by the government. The executive-legislative conflicts of the colonial period greatly influenced the form of government established. As a result, the legislature was put in control of all phases of government.[10] There were also executive and judicial branches established, but the General Assembly had the power to choose all executive officers, including the governor, and all the judges. The Constitution also left the design of the court system to the General Assembly. No system of local government was outlined, but there was provision for the offices of justice of the peace, sheriff, coroner and constable.

From the time of statehood, North Carolina had a bicameral legislature in which both houses were elected by the people. One representative was elected to the Senate from each county. The House of Commons was composed of two representatives from each county and one representative from each town listed in the Constitution.[11] Only landowners

9. *Ibid.*, p. 284.
10. Cheney, p. 283.
11. *Ibid.*, p. 284.

could vote for senators. Property qualifications applied to candidates for the General Assembly and governor.

The period from 1776 to 1835 has been described as one of little progress in North Carolina, but it was during that time that the permanent seat of government was moved from New Bern to the new city of Raleigh in 1792.

Government was controlled by the residents of the coastal plain area. Because representation was by governmental unit, the General Assembly leaders were reluctant to create new counties in the west as population grew there. When it became necessary to form a new county in the west, the General Assembly would divide one of the coastal plain counties at the same time. As a result, the eastern area continued to control the General Assembly.

The Constitutional Convention of 1835

Demands for reforms in the system of government finally resulted in the calling of a constitutional convention in 1835. The convention proposed amendments, subsequently adopted, that fixed the membership of the House at 120 and the Senate at 50 and that provided for the election of senators and representatives from districts based upon population.[12] Another amendment provided for the popular election of the governor for a two-year term, but the Assembly continued to elect all other state officials.

The Constitutional Conventions of 1861-62 and 1865-66

A secession act, adopted by delegates to a constitutional convention on May 20, 1861, took the state out of the Union and into the Confederacy. In the Civil War which followed, many lives were lost, and the resources of the state were destroyed. Slavery was abolished, and secession was nullified

12. *Ibid.*

by a convention five years later. A period of reconstruction partially under military supervision existed until 1877.

The Constitution of 1868

In 1868, a new Constitution was adopted as the state was readmitted to the Union. Changes included a new name for the House of Commons—to the House of Representatives—and election by the people of all state executive officers, judges and county officials. All executive officials were to be elected for four-year terms. Property qualifications for voting and holding elective office were abolished. Legislative sessions were to be held annually, and the lieutenant governor was made president of the Senate.[13]

Other provisions established a uniform court system, a system of taxation, support for free public schools and a uniform system of government for counties and towns.

Constitutional Changes from 1873 to 1971

Amendments to the Constitution between 1873 and 1900 restored the power of the General Assembly over local government and the courts. The General Assembly gained full power to revise or abolish the form and rights of county and township governments. Legislative sessions became biennial again. The simplicity and uniformity of the court system were altered when the General Assembly was given the power to determine the jurisdiction of all courts below the Supreme Court. The Supreme Court was reduced from five members to three, and superior court judges were required to rotate among all judicial districts of the state.

Among other amendments, persons found guilty of felonies were disqualified from voting. Public schools were required to provide equal opportunities for education, but on a racially segregated basis, a provision not included in the 1971 Constitution. In 1900 literacy tests and poll tax requirements for

13. *Ibid.*, p. 283.

voting were added and later removed. Also, the procedure for amending the Constitution was simplified.

By 1930 amendments had been adopted which authorized special superior court judges, limited the Assembly's power to levy taxes and to incur debt and reduced residency requirements for voters.

The Constitution of 1971

Following the recommendations of several constitutional study commissions, the 1969 General Assembly submitted to the voters a new Constitution. It was ratified Nov. 3, 1970, and went into effect July 1, 1971. Since then, 28 amendments have been submitted to the people and 23 have been ratified. Three amendments have had the most impact on state government: the 1970 amendment authorizing the governor to reorganize the executive branch; the 1977 amendment allowing the governor to seek a second, consecutive term and the amendment requiring the state to adopt a balanced budget, passed the same year.

The Executive Organization Acts of 1971 and 1973

By 1970, the government of the state involved several hundred thousand people in an administration which included over 200 independent state agencies. Steps toward reorganizing and reducing the number of these agencies—implementing the 1970 constitutional amendment—were taken by the Committee on State Government. The committee recommended a plan to the legislature which would group agencies together in a limited number of functional departments. The Executive Organization Act of 1971 (G.S. 143 A-1 *et. seq.*) created 19 principal offices and departments. These included the agencies headed by elected officials (the Council of State) and nine others formed by grouping agencies of similar function under a single administrative head appointed by the governor.

11

The 1973 act (G.S. 143B-1 *et. seq.*) improved the management and coordination of four state departments: the Departments of Human Resources, Cultural Resources, Military and Veterans Affairs—which later became Crime Control and Public Safety—and Revenue. The law established the powers of the secretaries, but left intact specifically designed areas and decisions already vested in various commissions which could not be countermanded by either the governor or a departmental secretary.[14]

The Governmental Evaluation Commission

A Governmental Evaluation Commission, also called the Sunset Commission, had a short life of four years in this state. The 1977 General Assembly passed a law establishing the commission to evaluate the performance of and to recommend the need for continued operation of more than 100 state regulatory agencies and programs, such as the boards governing watchmakers and water well contractors. The legislation provided a schedule for automatic termination of these programs and agencies unless the General Assembly voted to continue them. The commission, operating with staff independent of the General Assembly's Legislative Services Commission, was to recommend which agencies and programs should be changed or terminated. But in 1981, due to political pressure, financial considerations and criticism that the commission was moving too slowly and not accomplishing its purpose of reducing the size of government (only five boards had been recommended for termination), the General Assembly abolished the commission and transferred its unfinished business to a temporary legislative committee.

In Perspective

North Carolina government has been described in various ways throughout its history. In the early 1800s North Carolina was called the "Rip Van Winkle State" by critics who

14. *Ibid.*, p. 280.

said the state was undeveloped and backward, in addition to having a "general political apathy under a one-party system, which resulted in indifference to all cultural, social and economic matters."[15]

One of the most criticized features of North Carolina government throughout its history was the unequal representation in the General Assembly, weighted in favor of the eastern part of the state. When representation was by county, legislators dealt with the population movement westward by dividing an eastern county to offset the creation of a new county in the west. Even after 1835, when legislative seats were based upon population, representation was lopsided in favor of the east. As late as 1961, the 33 most populous counties had a representative for each 57,833 people, while the 12 least populous counties had a representative for each 7,065 people.[16] However, the "one man, one vote" U.S. Supreme Court decision and the 1965 Voting Rights Act forced changes toward more equitable representation.

Today, descriptions of the government are generally favorable. Political scientists writing in the *North Carolina Atlas* said it was the opinion of many students of state government that the state "enjoys reasonably good government."[17] It was described as "not spectacular," but "for the most part honest, efficient and effective."[18] Another political science professor has written that the "end result of government operations in North Carolina has been remarkably beneficial for its citizens."[19]

15. Lefler and Newsome, p. 314.
16. Lefler and Newsome, 2nd Ed., 1963, p. 634.
17. James W. Clay, Douglas M. Orr, Jr., and Alfred W. Stuart, *North Carolina Atlas*, (Chapel Hill: UNC Press, 1975), p. 70.
18. *Ibid.*
19. Richard H. Leach, "Book Tells Tar Heels About State," *Durham Morning Herald*, Jan. 16, 1977.

State Legislative Building—Raleigh

CHAPTER II

THE LEGISLATIVE BRANCH

Representative government officially began in North Carolina in 1665 with a unicameral (one-house) legislature.[1] Today the state's law-making body, the General Assembly, is composed of two houses: the Senate and the House of Representatives.

Members of both houses are elected from districts that are supposed to be divided as nearly equal as possible, according to population. The Senate's 50 members are elected from 32 Senate districts, and the 120 House members come from 53 districts, under the 1982 reapportionment plans. Districts are reapportioned by the General Assembly after every 10-year U.S. Census to insure that each representative will come from a district with approximately the same number of people as the next. The Constitution also stipulates that districts shall consist of contiguous territory and that no county shall be divided in the process of forming a district. However, the U.S. Department of Justice ruled in 1982 that prohibiting division of a county for redistricting is unconstitutional. Districts are to remain unchanged until the next decennial census. The General Assembly also apportions the districts for congressional representation.

Members of the House and Senate are elected to two-year terms. A constitutional amendment proposing that terms be changed to four years was defeated in June, 1982.

A senator must be 25 years old, a qualified voter and a resident of the state for two years and of the district for one year preceding election. A representative must be a qualified voter and a resident of the district for one year preceding election. If a vacancy occurs, the governor must appoint the

---

1. John L. Cheney, Jr. (Editor), *North Carolina Manual 1979*, (Raleigh: Office of the Secretary of State, 1979), p. 283.

SENATE DISTRICTS, 1982–

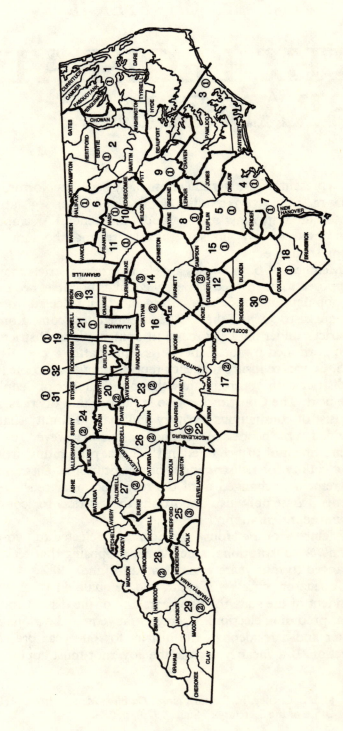

Number of senators per district is circled.

HOUSE OF REPRESENTATIVES DISTRICTS, 1982–

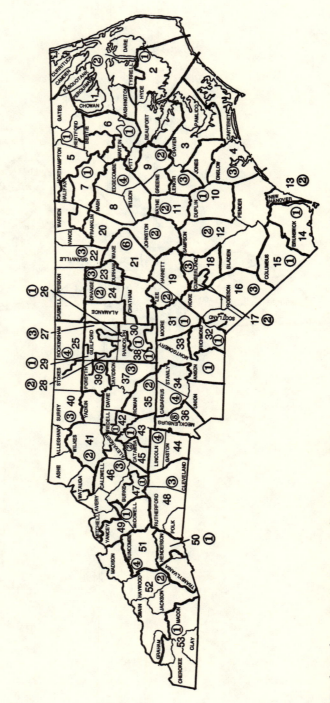

Number of representatives per district is circled.

CONGRESSIONAL

DISTRICTS, 1982–

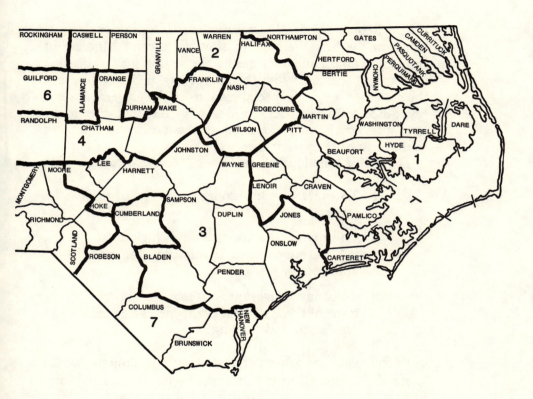

person recommended by the county executive committee of the vacating member's political party (G.S. 163-11).

How the General Assembly Works

The General Assembly convenes in odd-year biennial sessions on the first Wednesday after the second Monday in January. By parliamentary means, the session may be divided into annual segments with the time set by the Assembly, and the governor may call special sessions of the General Assembly. Since 1975, the General Assembly has met during the even-numbered years for a short session devoted almost exclusively to budgetary matters.

The major functions of the General Assembly are:

1. To enact laws governing the affairs of the state.

2. To provide and allocate funds for operating the government by enacting tax and appropriation laws.

3. To conduct investigations into such operations of the state as it deems necessary for regulation and funding.

By following procedures and constitutional limitations, the General Assembly can create new law and repeal old law. Generally, laws can be classified in five categories: (1) laws regulating individual conduct; (2) laws providing for services by the state; (3) laws empowering or directing local governments to act; (4) laws determining how much money shall be raised by the state and for what purposes it shall be spent and (5) amendments to the state Constitution.[2]

The Constitution lists 14 subjects on which the General Assembly is prohibited from enacting local, private or special acts or resolutions (Article II, Sec. 24, (1)).

2. *General Assembly of North Carolina*, (Raleigh: Legislative Services Office, undated) Chapter II.

The lieutenant governor presides over the Senate but only has a vote in case of a tie. The Senate elects a president pro tempore. The speaker of the House of Representatives is elected from its membership, as is the speaker pro tempore. The speaker votes with the membership or may delay his vote until the end to break a tie.

The speaker of the House and the president pro tempore of the Senate co-chair both the Legislative Services Commission and the Legislative Research Commission. Each appoints six members to the Services Commission which is the management authority for the General Assembly, providing such services as bill drafting, legal assistance, fiscal analysis and computer services. The two leaders also appoint five members from each body to serve on the Research Commission, which performs research projects for use in preparing legislation.

Each house elects officers which include the principal clerk, reading clerk and sergeant-at-arms.

As a general rule, the Senate and House meet in their respective chambers on Monday evenings, early afternoons on Tuesday through Thursday, and Friday mornings during the legislative session. Committee meetings are held in the mornings and late afternoons.

Legislative Committees

Much of the General Assembly's work is done in committees composed of members of the respective houses. Standing committees are enumerated in the rules adopted by each body for a session. Select or one-issue committees also are appointed as necessary. Some of the study committees function between sessions to carry on committee business and conduct related studies. Conference committees are appointed by the Senate and House leaders as needed to work on differences in adopted legislation.

The lieutenant governor, who appoints Senate committees, and the speaker, who appoints House committees, are considered especially powerful not only because they determine the composition of committees and their chairmen, but also because they assign proposed legislation to particular com-

21

mittees. Every legislator is appointed to serve on several different committees.

During the 1981 General Assembly session, the Senate had 38 standing committees, including agriculture, economy, election laws, public utilities, transportation, etc. The House had 58 standing committees, many duplicating the Senate list, but also including such titles as aging, corporations, governmental ethics, mental health, and water and air resources.[3]

In each body the base budget appropriations committees report on the money needed to continue existing state programs. The appropriations expansion budget committees decide how much money can be spent for expanding existing programs and for new programs that have been proposed. The finance committees deal with bond issues, methods for collecting taxes and any other matter affecting the state's or local government's taxing power. The Senate in recent years also established a Ways and Means Committee to have a final review power over bills assigned to the other money committees before the bills are considered on the Senate floor.[4]

Each house had three judiciary committees in 1981 to handle the large number of bills relating to civil and criminal court procedures and other legal matters.

Some of the committee assignments are especially prized by legislators because of the power that can be exerted with legislation the so-called "important" committees consider. Appropriations committees are generally considered the most powerful because they determine where money will be spent by the state. Other money committees, as well as those that regulate the large industries in North Carolina, such as banking and insurance, also have the unofficial tag of "important" committees.

How a Bill Becomes a Law

The process of making a new law begins when one or more legislators sponsor a legislative bill. Bills are generally drawn

3. *North Carolina General Assembly, Senate Rules-Directory* and *House Rules-Directory* (Raleigh: General Assembly, 1981), Senate Rule 32 and House Rule 27.
4. *Ibid.*, Senate Rule 41.1.

Organizational Chart
Legislative Branch

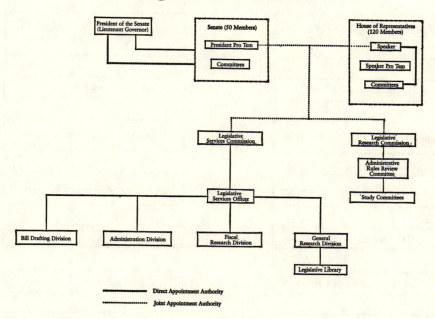

President of the Senate (Lieutenant Governor)	Senate (50 Members)	House of Representatives (120 Members)
	President Pro Tem	Speaker
	Committees	Speaker Pro Tem
		Committees

Legislative Services Commission

Legislative Research Commission

Administrative Rules Review Committee

Legislative Services Officer

Study Committees

Bill Drafting Division

Administration Division

Fiscal Research Division

General Research Division

Legislative Library

▬▬▬▬▬▬▬ Direct Appointment Authority

············· Joint Appointment Authority

MAJOR STEPS IN THE LEGISLATIVE PROCESS[1]

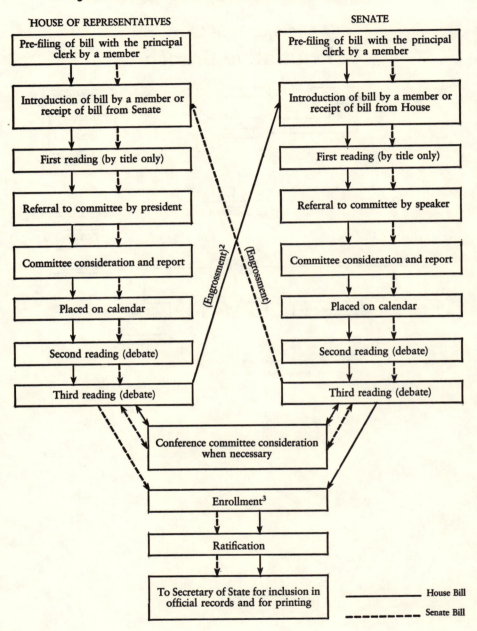

HOUSE OF REPRESENTATIVES

Pre-filing of bill with the principal clerk by a member

Introduction of bill by a member or receipt of bill from Senate

First reading (by title only)

Referral to committee by president

Committee consideration and report

Placed on calendar

Second reading (debate)

Third reading (debate)

SENATE

Pre-filing of bill with the principal clerk by a member

Introduction of bill by a member or receipt of bill from House

First reading (by title only)

Referral to committee by speaker

Committee consideration and report

Placed on calendar

Second reading (debate)

Third reading (debate)

(Engrossment)[2]

(Engrossment)

Conference committee consideration when necessary

Enrollment[3]

Ratification

To Secretary of State for inclusion in official records and for printing

—————— House Bill

-------- Senate Bill

[1]Adapted from a chart by Michael Crowell and Milton S. Heath, jr., *The General Assembly of North Carolina, A Handbook for Legislators* (Chapel Hill: Institute of Government), fourth edition, 1981, p. 56.

[2]Engrossment is the process of incorporating amendments into the original text of a bill.

[3]Enrollment is the process of retyping a bill in its final form before it is submitted to the presiding officers for their signatures.

up by drafting specialists in the Legislative Services Office who work with the legislators to see that the proposed bill meets standard requirements and is in the proper form. The attorney general's office, which has the statutory duty to draft bills for state departments and agencies, may also be used by legislators to prepare bills. When the bill has been prepared, it is ready for pre-filing which consists of giving a copy to the principal clerk on the day preceding the introduction of the bill. At the time reserved on the calendar for the introduction of bills, the reading clerk reads the title and its number, and the presiding officer assigns it to a committee. Thus the bill is introduced.

Bills may be introduced in either the House or the Senate, but must be approved in an agreed-to form by both houses in order to become law. Since only legislators may introduce bills, the governor and state department leaders must find a willing senator or representative to submit their proposals.

When a bill is introduced, it is then referred to an appropriate committee by the presiding officer of that house. The committee studies the bill and may conduct public hearings before it is returned to the house from which it originated with one of the following recommendations:

1. Favorable

2. Report without prejudice (considered favorable) (an option only in the House)[5]

3. Postponed indefinitely (considered unfavorable)

4. Unfavorable

5. Unfavorable as to the bill but favorable as to a committee substitute prepared by the committee.

Sometimes the committee will report a bill without prejudice, or a minority report may accompany an unfavorable recommendation. If the minority report is signed by at least

5. *Ibid.*, House Rule 36(b).

one-fourth of the members of the committee who were present and voting when the bill was considered in committee, there may be a vote taken on the floor. If it then passes by a two-thirds majority of those present, the bill is placed on the favorable calendar for consideration.[6]

If the bill is reported with a favorable recommendation by the committee, it is then considered on the floor of the house where it was introduced. The Constitution requires that all bills be read three times in each house and voted on at each reading. The introduction of a bill constitutes its first reading. The second and third readings occur after the bill has been reported favorably out of committee. The second and third readings cannot be on the same day unless so ordered by a two-thirds majority of the members of that house who are present.[7]

The principal debate on the bill and consideration of germane amendments take place on the second reading and may occur again on the third reading. When the debate ends, the bill (with any amendments that have been adopted during the debate) is voted on, either by electronic voting system or by voice vote as determined by the rules of each house. The presiding officer declares the bill to have passed or failed on the basis of the required number of votes, and it is then sent to the other house for consideration.

It goes through the same procedure in each house of the General Assembly and must be passed in identical form or a form which is approved by a conference committee made up of members of both the House and the Senate. If the conference committee cannot agree, or if either house rejects the conference committee recommendation, the bill is defeated.

The final action in the passage of a bill is called ratification. This is the procedure in which the enrolled bill is signed by the presiding officers of both houses. The bill then becomes a state law and is delivered to the secretary of state, the custodian of the laws of the state.

The legislature considers resolutions in the same manner as bills, except that resolutions on merely ceremonial matters are often voted upon on the day of introduction without

6. *Ibid.*, Senate Rule 46(b); House Rule 36(e).
7. *Ibid.*, Senate Rule 50; House Rule 41(b).

committee review. Resolutions typically deal with organizational matters, recognize some important event or person or declare the position of the General Assembly on matters not subject to legislation.

The General Assembly is sometimes referred to as the most powerful of all state legislatures because North Carolina is the only state in which the governor does not have the power to veto legislation.

Legislative Agents

A legislative agent (lobbyist) is a person who attempts to influence specific legislation through personal appeals to legislators. Lobbyists may provide information, testify and solicit votes as individuals or at the direction of an organization or other group. If a lobbyist is paid to perform services, he or she is required to register, pay a fee and report the amount of money spent for lobbying to the secretary of state (G.S. 120-47.1).

Being a legislative agent may be a full-time, paid position or be incidental to other company or agency assignments. Although public officials are generally exempted from the registration and reporting requirements, the governor, all Council of State officers and all appointed heads of state agencies are required to file and report.

There are no registration or fee requirements for a citizen who wishes to lobby his own representative or for volunteers who work on behalf of organizations and associations.

ORGANIZATIONAL CHART OF
NORTH CAROLINA STATE GOVERNMENT

Issued By
THAD EURE, Secretary of State

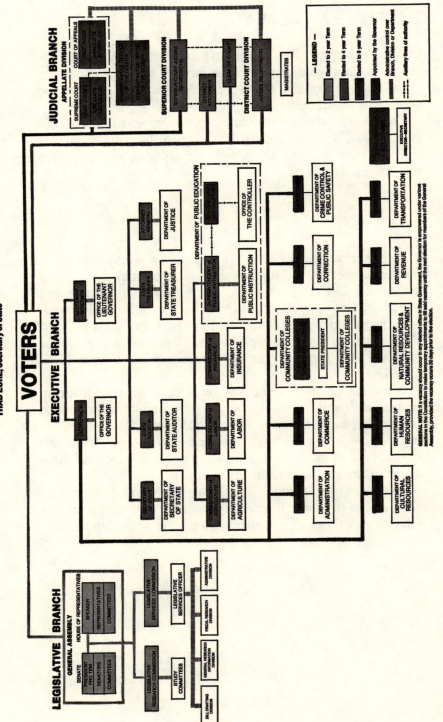

CHAPTER III

THE EXECUTIVE BRANCH

The branch of government charged with carrying out the duties and functions assigned by the legislature has grown from a "small, ill-funded endeavor of a few hundred 'employees' in 1776 to a multi-billion dollar enterprise"[1] of some 180,500 employees.

At the time the Constitution of 1971 was adopted, voters also approved an amendment which required a reduction in the number of state administrative departments and the streamlining of the state departments and agencies. The Executive Organization Acts of 1971 and 1973, carrying out the constitutional provisions, established 19 different offices in the executive branch. A twentieth department was created in 1979 when the Department of Community Colleges was separated from the Department of Public Education.

Ten offices were specifically named in the Constitution. The heads of each of those offices are elected statewide to four-year terms and constitute the Council of State. They are:

1. Governor

2. Lieutenant Governor

3. Secretary of State

4. State Auditor

5. State Treasurer

6. Superintendent of Public Instruction

7. Attorney General

8. Commissioner of Agriculture

---

1. John L. Cheney, Jr. (Editor), *North Carolina Manual 1979*, (Raleigh: Office of the Secretary of State, 1979), p. 279.

9. Commissioner of Labor

10. Commissioner of Insurance

Nine other executive departments were created and later reorganized. They are directed by secretaries who are appointed by the governor and serve as a cabinet at the governor's pleasure. The department secretaries are:

1. Secretary of Administration

2. Secretary of Commerce

3. Secretary of Correction

4. Secretary of Crime Control and Public Safety

5. Secretary of Cultural Resources

6. Secretary of Human Resources

7. Secretary of Natural Resources and Community Development

8. Secretary of Revenue

9. Secretary of Transportation

The tenth executive department, the Department of Community Colleges, is headed by a president who is appointed by the State Board of Community Colleges and is independent of the governor regarding actions and responsibilities.

Some 400 boards and commissions are under the jurisdiction of the various departments. Most are statutory bodies (established by the General Assembly), although some have been created by the governor and department heads. The power of each board and commission varies considerably, ranging from purely ceremonial or advisory to independent authority. Some oversee specific programs, such as one historical monument; others recommend policies to department secretaries; and a few set policies and regulations officials are obligated to follow.

THE EXECUTIVE BRANCH

Council of State Offices

Many Council of State offices have been a part of the executive branch since North Carolina government was in its formative stages. These long-established offices are fairly autonomous agencies since the leaders of each are elected, and their duties and functions are prescribed by the General Assembly. While a governor may make suggestions for procedures and programs in Council of State offices, it is not generally considered the governor's prerogative to reorganize those offices in the way he has power to do in the administrative departments.

The Council of State grouping, according to Milton S. Heath, Jr., of the Institute of Government, serves as a "mechanism to bring together" all of the elected executive branch officials to deal with common concerns and review problems in executive organization.

The Council of State as a whole has numerous duties and meets once a month at the call of the governor, who is the constitutionally designated chairman. The General Assembly has attached the requirement of Council of State approval to a long list of the governor's responsibilities. The list includes purchasing and selling state lands, borrowing money in anticipation of the collection of taxes, dedicating land to the state nature and historic preserve, allowing assessments against lands owned by the state, signing state bonds, spending money for emergencies and approving liquidation proceedings of banks.

Office of the Governor

The governor is the state's chief executive officer with the responsibility of "faithfully" executing all laws.[2] He is the chief budget officer of the state, according to the Constitution, with responsibility to prepare and recommend a budget of anticipated revenue and proposed expenditures to the General Assembly and then to administer the budget that is adopted. The Office of Budget and Management in the

---

2. *Constitution of the State of North Carolina* (as of July, 1980), Article III, Sec. 5(4).

governor's office handles these budgetary functions. The governor also is responsible for administration of all funds and loans from the federal government.

The Constitution establishes the governor as commander-in-chief of the state's military forces. Other constitutional powers and duties include delivering legislative and budgetary messages to the legislators, convening the General Assembly in extra sessions in emergencies with the advice of the Council of State, granting reprieves, commutations and pardons (except in cases of impeachment) and making appointments.

While North Carolina's chief executive has very strong appointment power—the authority to name some 4,000 persons to official positions on more than 400 boards and commissions[3] and in the judicial system, the governor is very weak in relations with the legislature. Today, the North Carolina governor is the only governor who does not have any veto power.

Powers of the executive during colonial times were weakened considerably at the writing of the first N.C. Constitution when it was mandated that the governor be elected by the two houses of the legislature. The Constitution has always provided for the executive, legislative and judicial branches to be "forever separate and distinct,"[4] but the General Assembly has acted throughout the state's history to restrict executive power. For example, the Advisory Budget Commission was created to help control executive budget preparation and to decide which purchase contracts would be awarded. A Governmental Operations Commission was established to provide legislative scrutiny of tax expenditures and later was given the power to approve certain budget transfers as the budget was administered. The legislature has put its members on more than 44 of the governor's boards and commissions. In the 1981 legislative session, the governor had to fight off an attempt by the General Assembly to gain a "legislative veto" over rules drawn up by executive branch agencies.

---

3. Thad L. Beyle, "How Powerful is the North Carolina Governor?" *N.C. Insight*, Vol. 4, No. 4, (December, 1981), p. 5.
4. *Constitution*, Article I, Sec. 6.

Lawmakers compromised with an act that allows objection, but still gives the governor the final word.

The Office of the Governor has several sections and assistants to help in the administration of the state's business. The titles and numbers of advisers and assistants usually change with each new governor. Among those that have been used are the special assistant for minority affairs, special assistant for education, special assistant for federal-state relations, legal counsel, legislative counsel, press officer, director of an Office of Citizen Affairs and science and public policy adviser.

Occasionally a governor will set up a special section in an administrative department or in his office to carry out a program of special interest that might normally fall under a Council of State office. For example, Gov. Jim Hunt appointed a special assistant for education to promote a statewide reading and testing program in the public schools. Gov. James Holshouser established an Office of Ombudsman to receive citizen complaints and provide information and referral.

To be eligible for election to the position of governor or lieutenant governor, a person must be 30 years old, a U.S. citizen for five years and a North Carolina resident for the two years immediately preceding election.

Other boards and commissions under the jurisdiction of the Office of the Governor are:

> Advisory Council to the Governor's Office of
>   Citizen Affairs
> Council on Volunteers for the Criminal
>   Justice System
> N.C. Local Government Advocacy Council
> Judicial Nominating Committee for Superior
>   Court Judges

Office of the Lieutenant Governor

The lieutenant governor serves as president of the North Carolina Senate and, in that position, appoints Senate committees and their chairmen and assigns bills to committees. Related responsibilities include supervising the staff of pages, sergeant-at-arms and various clerks. The lieutenant governor also performs any duties that the governor may assign and is acting governor in the absence of the governor.

The lieutenant governor is a member of the following governmental boards and commissions:

> State Board of Education
> Land Policy Council
> Commission on Interstate Cooperation
> Commission on Indian Affairs
> North Carolina Capital Planning Commission
> Governmental Operations Committee
> State Board of Community Colleges
> N.C. Economic Development Board
> Commission on the Future

Office of the Secretary of State

The right of citizens to information about their government is the basis for the functions of the Office of the Secretary of State. The office has responsibilities under some 50 different state statutes which generally fall into the following categories:[5]

1. Custodianship of the Constitution and laws of the state.

2. Administrative commercial law.

3. Elective process.

4. General Assembly.

5. Public information.

The secretary of state convenes the House of Representatives and presides over it until a speaker is elected, assigns seats to members of the House, preserves the original journals of the House and Senate and attends every session of the legislature to receive bills which have been passed. The registration and supervision of lobbyists at the General Assembly is the responsibility of the secretary of state.

5. Cheney, p. 459.

THE EXECUTIVE BRANCH

Other duties of the office include administering oaths to public officials, registering trademarks, filing municipal annexation ordinances, maintaining records of registered corporations, issuing commissions to notaries public and keeping all records available for public information. These duties are divided among the secretary, deputy secretary, Corporation Division, Uniform Commercial Code Division, Securities Division, Notary Public Division and Publications Division.

The Publications Division compiles and publishes information useful to the General Assembly, state agencies and the public, including:

> *North Carolina Manual*
> *Session Laws*
> *House and Senate Journals*
> *Directory of State and County Officials*
> *Directory of State Governmental Services*

Office of the State Auditor

The Office of the State Auditor conducts annual audits of the financial affairs of all state agencies, checking accounts and records. Other special audits may be requested by the Advisory Budget Commission and the governor or be initiated by the state auditor. The office also conducts operational audits of selected programs administered by state agencies to determine that the programs are accomplishing the desired results in an efficient and effective manner.

The auditor also administers the Firemen's Pension Fund and the State Board of Pensions.

In addition to being the state's financial watchdog, the state auditor is chairman of the Firemen's Pension Fund and a member of the Capital Planning Commission, the Local Government Commission, the State Pension Board and the Law Enforcement Officers' Benefit and Retirement Fund.

Independent of any fiscal control exercised by the governor, the auditor is responsible to the Advisory Budget Commission and General Assembly.

NORTH CAROLINA: OUR STATE GOVERNMENT

Office of the State Treasurer

The state treasurer is responsible for the receipt, custody and disbursement of all state funds, including the supervision of investment of funds not needed immediately to meet obligations of the state government. The treasurer serves as fiscal consultant to the governor, the General Assembly and the Advisory Budget Commission. Through the Local Government Commission, the treasurer also serves as fiscal consultant to local governments. Management of state funds is vested in a system of checks and balances through the coordinated efforts of the treasurer, the director of the budget and the state auditor.

The state treasurer also invests money that is in the state's six retirement systems and the Escheat Fund, which uses dividends from the investment of unclaimed property to help needy North Carolina college students.

The department's activities are handled by its four divisions:

> Division of Investment and Banking
> Division of State and Local Government Finance
> Division of Retirement and Health Benefits
> Division of Administrative Services

The treasurer is chairman of the Tax Review Board and the State Banking Commission and is a member of the State Board of Education, the Capital Planning Commission, the North Carolina Capital Building Authority and the Board of Trustees of the Retirement Systems.

Other boards under the jurisdiction of the Office of the state treasurer include:

> North Carolina Local Government
>   Employee's Retirement System
> Municipal Board of Control
> Revenue Sharing Advisory Committee

THE EXECUTIVE BRANCH

Department of Public Education

The Department of Public Education is actually headed by the State Board of Education. The elected superintendent of public instruction serves as the board's secretary and chief administrative officer. While the board has no voice in the superintendent's selection, the official must act according to the board's directions. Board members include the lieutenant governor, state treasurer and 11 members appointed to eight-year terms by the governor and confirmed by the General Assembly.

It is the board's function, under the Constitution, to supervise and administer the free public school system, grades K-12, and the educational funds provided for its support. The board establishes general regulations and policies under which local boards of education operate, and it disburses the funds appropriated for the state's 1.2 million students. Specific responsibilities of the state board include certifying teachers, adopting and supplying textbooks, adopting a standard course of study, operating a state insurance system and submitting a proposed budget for the public schools to the General Assembly. Local boards of education make policy and give direction at the city or county level within State Board of Education guidelines. Local school districts may supplement state funds with county taxes.

The Department of Public Education is organized to handle six broad functions: administrative services, instructional services, student services, personnel relations, research and development and teacher education.

Within the department, educational leadership and management programs are developed and directed to strengthen administration on all levels of public education. Instructional services, in such areas as math, English, science, music and physical education, range from providing assistance in planning, implementing and evaluating programs to developing curriculum materials and conducting workshops for staff development. Eight regional education centers offer various support services to local school administrators and teachers.

The Division for Exceptional Children develops programs and services for children with special needs, including those who are autistic, gifted and talented, hearing impaired, men-

Department

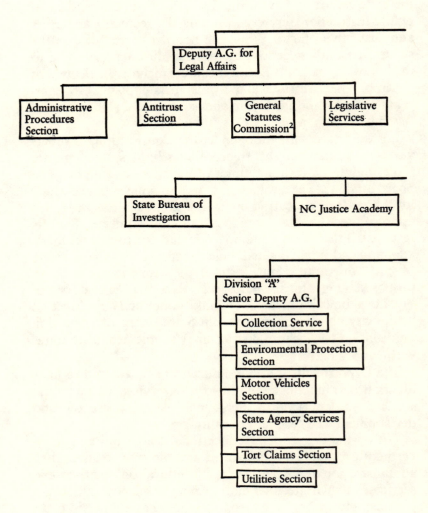

Deputy A.G. for
Legal Affairs

Administrative
Procedures
Section

Antitrust
Section

General
Statutes
Commission[2]

Legislative
Services

State Bureau of
Investigation

NC Justice Academy

Division "A"
Senior Deputy A.G.

Collection Service

Environmental Protection
Section

Motor Vehicles
Section

State Agency Services
Section

Tort Claims Section

Utilities Section

# of Justice

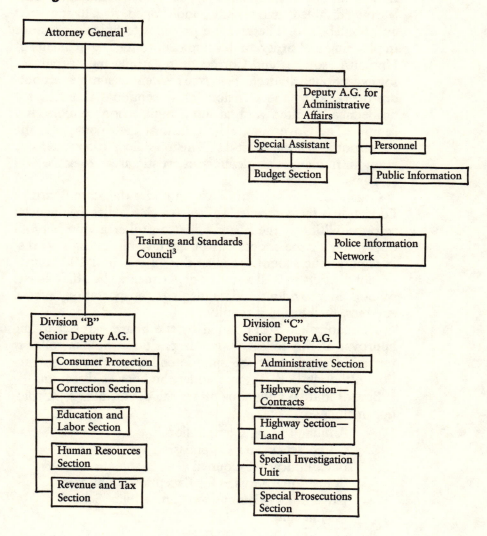

Attorney General[1]

Deputy A.G. for Administrative Affairs

Special Assistant

Budget Section

Personnel

Public Information

Training and Standards Council[3]

Police Information Network

Division "B"
Senior Deputy A.G.

Consumer Protection

Correction Section

Education and Labor Section

Human Resources Section

Revenue and Tax Section

Division "C"
Senior Deputy A.G.

Administrative Section

Highway Section—Contracts

Highway Section—Land

Special Investigation Unit

Special Prosecutions Section

[1] Elected by the People
[2] Department provides full-time staff to the Commission. The Governor does not appoint a majority of the Commission's members.
[3] Department provides full-time staff to the Council. The Governor does not appoint a majority of the Council's members.

tally handicapped, multihandicapped, speech impaired, specific learning disabled, emotionally handicapped, visually impaired and homebound. The division provides technical assistance in planning and program development to the Departments of Human Resources and Correction regarding their programs for exceptional children. Two free residential summer schools are operated by the Division for Exceptional Children for academically gifted and talented high school juniors and seniors. The Governor's School East at Laurinburg and the Governor's School West at Winston-Salem offer intensive study in numerous academic and artistic areas to some 400 students annually.

Organized as a separate division under the State Board of Education is the controller's office, which handles the financial responsibilities of the board. The controller administers all operations in the process of budgeting, allocating and disbursing public school funds to the 43 city and 100 county school districts as well as to the department. The office assists schools in providing and managing transportation, school supplies, facilities and textbooks.

The controller is appointed by the board, subject to the approval of the governor. In the position, the controller is fairly independent of the superintendent of public instruction, although both operate under the board's direction.

Boards and commissions under the department's jurisdiction include:

Annual Testing Commission
Competency Test Commission
N.C. Education Council
Educational Services for Exceptional Children
Governor's Commission on Public School
    Financing
N.C. Textbook Commission
N.C. Advisory Council on Education

Department of Justice

The Department of Justice serves as the "people's attorney," protecting individual rights as guaranteed by the North Carolina and United States Constitutions. The attorney general is the elected head of the Department of Justice which includes the State Bureau of Investigation, the Police Information Network, the N.C. Criminal Justice Academy, the N.C. Criminal Justice Standards Division and a deputy attorney general's office for administrative affairs. The attorney general serves as an ex officio member of numerous state boards and commissions.

The attorney general's responsibilities generally are in two major areas: legal services and law enforcement.

The Office of the Attorney General is the legal firm for the state and handles all legal matters of its departments, divisions and agencies. The attorney general reviews the legality of forms and contracts used by state agencies, investigates claims in which state agencies are involved and prepares forms for the acquisition and disposition of real property for the state. Staff attorneys are assigned to represent the state on appeals to the N.C. Court of Appeals, the N.C. Supreme Court, the U.S. District Court, the U.S. Court of Appeals and the U.S. Supreme Court.

The attorney general provides opinions, either formally or informally, on questions of law submitted by the General Assembly, the governor or any other state officer. The attorney general also consults with judges, district attorneys and other local legal officials when requested and intervenes in or initiates proceedings before any court or regulatory body, state or federal, on behalf of the people of the state.

Laws and procedures are reviewed by the Office of the Attorney General, and recommendations for changes may be made. This office is responsible for the codification of all laws enacted by the General Assembly. It also maintains a bill drafting office to assist state officials and legislators in preparing legislation.

The department's services to local government include litigation of claims in which injuries have been caused by school buses and advice to county boards of election, state and local ABC officials, county medical examiners and other local government officials.

Other concerns of the attorney general are consumer protection, antitrust matters, unfair trade practices and Utilities Commission proceedings.

The State Bureau of Investigation assists in administering criminal laws of the state through crime prevention programs and apprehension of criminals. The Bureau's highest priorities are investigating and solving violent crimes such as murder, rape, armed robbery, arson and hard drug trafficking.

The Bureau assists local law enforcement in the investigation of criminals, the scientific analysis of the evidence of crimes and the investigation and preparation of evidence to be used in court.

Other boards and commissions under the department's jurisdiction are:

Criminal Code Commission
General Statutes Commission
Private Protective Services Board

North Carolina Tobacco Barns

THE EXECUTIVE BRANCH

Department of Agriculture

The Department of Agriculture always has had responsibility for research in and promotion of North Carolina's agricultural products. In recent years, however, the department has been expanded considerably to include consumer protection responsibilities. It is in charge of the enforcement of many regulatory programs which protect and promote the health, safety and welfare of all citizens.

Heading the department is an elected commissioner of agriculture who directs the implementation of more than 75 different laws and programs. To carry out these functions, the department is divided into four main program areas: administration, agricultural services and development, consumer protection and education and research.

Farmers are helped by the department through technical assistance programs, marketing aids and a commodities storage system. A statistics section provides information, such as farm income and wages, which helps farmers decide whether to increase or decrease production of specific crops or livestock. The state veterinarian's office is involved in the prevention, control and eradication of infectious diseases of livestock and poultry, and the Division of Plant Industry works to prevent and control plant pests. Seed and soil testing are other department services.

The Division of Research operates 15 research stations at Whiteville, Clinton, Waynesville, Oxford, Lewiston, Salisbury, Plymouth, Rocky Mount, Laurel Springs, Clayton, Castle Hayne, Kinston, Fletcher, Jackson Springs and Reidsville. The farms are intended to develop new varieties of crops and livestock and techniques of production to make farming more efficient, productive and profitable.

Inspections, laboratory analyses and other regulatory activities are performed through consumer protection programs in the department. Some of these activities include analyzing foods, dairy products, drugs and cosmetics for wholesomeness, sanitation and proper labeling; checking the quality of feeds, seeds, fertilizers and pesticides; enforcing the weights and measures law; inspecting the quality and quantity of gasoline and oil products; setting safety standards for use of pesticides and licensing pest control businesses.

43

The department also is responsible for operating regional farmers' markets, two horse show arenas, the North Carolina Museum of Natural History and the State Fair.

The commissioner of agriculture is ex officio chairman of the Board of Agriculture, the State Board of Gasoline and Oil Inspection and the North Carolina Agricultural Hall of Fame board. The commissioner is an ex officio member of the following:

Crop Seed Improvement Board
Atomic Energy Advisory Committee
Agriculture Foundation Board of Directors
Cotton Promotion Committee
N.C. Board of Farm Organizations and
    Agencies
N.C. Committee on Migrant Labor
Governor's Council on Occupational Health
N.C. Council on Food and Nutrition
N.C. Veterinary School Selection Committee
N.C. Rural Rehabilitation Corporation Board
    of Directors

Other boards and commissions under the jurisdiction of the Department of Agriculture are:

Advisory Commission for the Museum of
    Natural History
N.C. Pesticide Board/N.C. Pesticide Advisory
    Committee
Structural Pest Control Committee
N.C. Plant Conservation Board
Plant Conservation Scientific Committee
State Farm Operations Committee
N.C. Public Livestock Market Board

Department of Labor

The Department of Labor, under the direction of the elected commissioner of labor, is responsible for promoting the health, safety and general well-being of the state's more than three million working people. State laws provide the commissioner with broad regulatory and enforcement powers with which to carry out his duties. Several of the department's functions involve cooperation and close working relationships with other state and federal agencies.

The principal regulatory, enforcement and promotional programs of the Department of Labor are carried out by nine divisions. Brief descriptions of the divisions follow.

1. The Apprenticeship Division administers and monitors a broad range of apprenticeship and on-the-job training programs in the skilled trades. The division promotes programs with individual employers and with joint labor-management committees to train workers on the job and provide related technical training in nearby community colleges.

2. The Boiler and Pressure Vessel Division inspects boilers and pressure vessels operated in the state and maintains records concerning the ownership, location and condition of each.

3. The Conciliation and Arbitration Division mediates labor-management problems.

4. The Elevator Division inspects elevators, dumbwaiters, moving walks, aerial passenger tramways and a variety of amusement devices and special equipment for safety.

5. The Mine and Quarry Division conducts a broad program of inspections, training and consultations to implement provisions of the Mine Safety and Health Act.

6. The Occupational Safety and Health Division administers the act (OSHA) which sets safety and health standards for most private sector employment and agriculture. The division offers free consultative services, education, and training in safety and

45

health on the job and inspects labor sites for compliance with the law.

7. The Private Employment Agencies Division investigates, licenses and regulates all private employment agencies operating in the state.

8. The Research and Statistics Division compiles and publishes comprehensive data on occupational injuries and illness in North Carolina.

9. The Wage and Hour Division enforces the N.C. Wage and Hour Act which has provisions governing youth employment, minimum wages, maximum working hours, overtime pay and uniform wage payment.

Several labor-related activities are found in other state departments. For example, the unemployment insurance program and labor market statistical information are handled by the Department of Commerce. State CETA (Comprehensive Employment and Training Act) operations are supervised by the Department of Natural Resources and Community Development. Vocational rehabilitation is the responsibility of the Department of Human Resources.

North Carolina does not have a state law prohibiting discrimination in employment. The U.S. Equal Employment Opportunity Commission office in Charlotte is the enforcement agency for federal laws regarding discrimination in employment in the state.

Boards and councils which assist the Department of Labor are:

Apprenticeship Advisory Council
Board of Boiler and Pressure Vessel Rules
Mine Safety and Health Advisory Council
Occupational Safety and Health Advisory
    Council
Industry Advisory Board

THE EXECUTIVE BRANCH

An independent board, the Occupational Safety and Health Review Board, is appointed by the governor to hear appeals concerning citations and penalties imposed by the Occupational Safety and Health Division.

Department of Insurance

The elected commissioner of insurance has primary responsibility for the execution of laws regarding insurance. These duties include licensing and supervising insurance companies and protecting the holders of insurance policies.

The department is divided into 11 divisions to carry out its activities. Brief descriptions of the divisions follow.

1. The Fire and Rescue Training Division administers the Firemen's Relief Fund, develops and carries out training for fire departments and rescue squads and works to improve fire and rescue protection procedures in the state.

2. The Consumer Insurance Information Division responds to questions and complaints from the public. A toll-free telephone number is listed in Appendix A.

3. The Engineers and Building Codes Division enforces state building codes in cooperation with local officials and supervises the inspection of manufacturers of mobile homes and manufactured buildings.

4. The Licensing Division regulates and annually licenses every agent, adjuster, broker and appraiser doing insurance business in North Carolina.

5. The Fire and Casualty Division examines and recommends rates, policy forms and rules for fidelity and surety bonds and for fire, auto, inland marine, workmen's compensation, aviation, burglary and theft,

liability, glass, boiler and machinery and title insurance.

6. The State Property Fire Insurance Fund insures state-owned buildings, approves plans and inspects them.

7. The Investigations Division conducts criminal investigations dealing with embezzlement and insurance fraud.

8. The Company Operations Division supervises all domestic and foreign insurance organizations not based in the state but doing business in North Carolina.

9. The Administrative Law Division conducts administrative hearings on rates, license revocations, and other practices.

10. The Special Service Division licenses and regulates bail bondsmen, collection agencies and motor clubs and investigates citizen complaints regarding them.

11. The Administration Division provides administrative services.

Boards under the jursidiction of the department are:
Building Code Council
Health Insurance Advisory Board
Insurance Advisory Board
N.C. Code Officials Qualification Board
Health Care Excess Liability Fund Board

Executive Departments

The nine administrative departments that make up the governor's cabinet were formed by grouping the numerous agencies and programs outside the ten Council of State offices along functional lines.[6] Under the reorganization amendment to the Constitution, the governor can create up to 25 administrative departments. Administrative departments can be created or reorganized by executive order, which stands unless the General Assembly acts to rescind or amend it.

Since the department secretaries are appointed by the governor and serve only as long as the governor approves, the secretaries have a much closer working relationship with the governor than do the Council of State officers. Programs and policies reflect the governor's personal and political priorities to a great extent.

The secretaries as a group are called the cabinet. They meet weekly and sometimes more often with the governor. The secretaries and Council of State officers meet as an executive cabinet with the governor once every two weeks.

Department of Administration

The Department of Administration is the business and management office of state government, providing support and services to other offices in the government. It handles matters of personnel, property maintenance, purchasing, computer services and building design and construction, among others. It is the liaison between the state and federal government. The department generally manages the state's in-house affairs and helps the governor coordinate the work of all state agencies.

The secretary of administration prepares the agenda and serves as staff for all meetings of the Council of State. It is the secretary's responsibility to implement the actions recommended by the Council of State, the Advisory Budget Commission and the Capital Planning Commission. The secretary is chairman of the Capital Building Authority.

The Office of Policy and Planning coordinates interdepartmental program planning and serves as policy staff to the governor. The department also serves as the home agency of several advocacy programs for special public interest groups such as women, minorities, children, the disabled, young people and Indians.

6. *Ibid.*, p. 280.

Boards under the jurisdiction of the Department of Administration include:

> Capital Building Authority
> Capital Planning Commission
> Council on the Status of Women
> Human Relations Council
> State Commission of Indian Affairs
> Governor's Advocacy Council on Children and Youth
> Veterans Affairs Commission
> Advisory Committee on Land Records
> Marine Resources Center Administrative Board
> Advocacy Council for the Mentally Ill and Developmentally Disabled
> N.C. State Goals and Policy Board
> N.C. School of Science and Mathematics Board of Trustees
> Marine Science Council

Department of Commerce

The Department of Commerce is responsible for promoting economic development in North Carolina, managing energy resources, operating the State Ports Authority at Morehead City and Wilmington and overseeing administrative matters for ten regulatory and public service agencies. The department, headed by the secretary of commerce, also supervises the Employment Security Commission which administers the state's unemployment insurance program, prepares labor market statistical information and operates job referral and job development programs.

The Economic Development Program promotes and assists expansion in industry, travel, food production, international trade and reverse investment in order to improve the economy of the state. The industrial development and international divisions recruit industry to build in this state. An export development program matches North Carolina suppliers with overseas buyers.

The Business Assistance Division helps existing businesses. That help takes many forms, including staffing the Small

Business Advocacy Council, providing financial and management advice to companies, assisting minority businesses and administering the state industrial revenue bond program.

The Travel and Tourism Division promotes the state's attractions to vacationers, convention planners and writers and operates welcome centers on the major highways. The division annually issues a free brochure listing day-by-day events throughout the state for the calendar year. It is available by writing to the division in the Department of Commerce (address in Appendix A).

A separate N.C. Film Office was created to promote the state as a site for making motion pictures.

A recent addition to the Department of Commerce is the Energy Division. It was created to develop programs to handle energy emergencies, conservation and allocation. It also administers specialty programs for conserving energy in schools and hospitals, weatherizing homes, developing alternate energy sources and educating the public on such subjects as wood energy and solar power.

Regulatory agencies, exercising quasi-legislative and quasi-judicial authority, each operate independently of the department. The department's only role is to coordinate management functions and perform administrative services. Brief descriptions of the regulatory agencies follow.

1. The State Commission of Alcoholic Control is responsible for controlling all aspects of the sale and distribution of alcoholic beverages in North Carolina. The state's Alcohol Beverage Control (ABC) system is unique in that there are over 145 separate county and municipal ABC boards. Each board is responsible for the sale of alcoholic beverages in its county or city as determined by a vote of the residents. The commission controls the shipment of liquor, beer and wine into the state and is responsible for distribution to the local boards. The ABC commission has three members, all appointed by the governor.

Department of Commerce

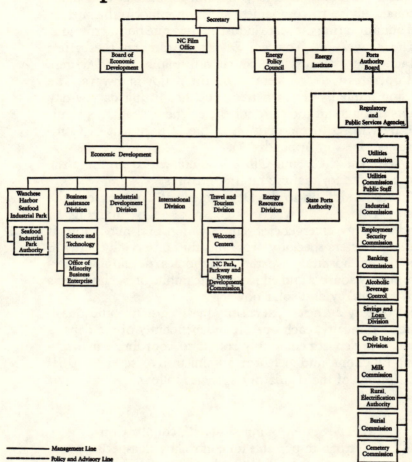

Secretary

NC Film Office

Board of Economic Development

Energy Policy Council

Energy Institute

Ports Authority Board

Regulatory and Public Services Agencies

Economic Development

Wanchese Harbor Seafood Industrial Park

Business Assistance Division

Industrial Development Division

International Division

Travel and Tourism Division

Energy Resources Division

State Ports Authority

Seafood Industrial Park Authority

Science and Technology

Office of Minority Business Enterprise

Welcome Centers

NC Park, Parkway and Forest Development Commission

Utilities Commission

Utilities Commission Public Staff

Industrial Commission

Employment Security Commission

Banking Commission

Alcoholic Beverage Control

Savings and Loan Division

Credit Union Division

Milk Commission

Rural Electrification Authority

Burial Commission

Cemetery Commission

———— Management Line
- - - - Policy and Advisory Line

2. The Banking Commission regulates and supervises the activities of more than 1,500 financial institutions chartered under N.C. laws. The commission examines all state-chartered banks and consumer finance licensees and processes applications for new banks, branch banks and licenses. Twelve members of this commission are appointed by the governor for four-year terms; the state treasurer serves ex officio.

3. The Burial Commission supervises and audits mutual burial associations in the state. The commission has five members, four elected by the Burial Association and one appointed by the governor.

4. The Cemetery Commission regulates privately owned cemeteries. The governor appoints four members, and three others are elected by the commission.

5. The Credit Union Commission supervises and regulates the operation of state-chartered credit unions. Seven members are appointed by the governor; the secretary of commerce serves ex officio as chairman.

6. The Industrial Commission administers the Workman's Compensation Act and has jurisdiction over death claims filed by dependents of firemen, rescue squad members and law enforcement officers who die in the line of duty. The commission also hears cases filed against the state by persons who are injured due to a negligent act by a state employee. Three members, appointed by the governor, serve six-year terms.

7. The Milk Commission is primarily responsible for assuring that an ade-

quate supply of wholesome milk is available for the state's citizens by regulating production, marketing and distribution. This includes establishing the wholesale price for milk. Members serve four-year terms and are appointed as follows: two by the lieutenant governor, two by the speaker of the House, three by the commissioner of agriculture and three by the governor.

8. The Rural Electrification Authority supervises 28 electric membership corporations and nine telephone membership corporations in the state to see that they apply their rules and regulations fairly. It investigates complaints, provides technical assistance and approves local applications for federal loans. The governor appoints six members to four-year terms.

9. The Savings and Loan Commission supervises the operation of state-chartered savings and loan associations to protect the interests of borrowers, savers and the general public. Seven members are appointed by the governor.

10. The N.C. Utilities Commission is responsible for maintaining an efficient system of utilities by fixing and regulating rates, conducting formal hearings and issuing written decisions. It also investigates customer complaints regarding utility operations and services. The commission has jurisdiction over public electric, telephone, natural gas, water and sewer companies, passenger carriers, freight carriers and railroads. The governor appoints seven

members, with the approval of the General Assembly, to eight-year terms.

In 1977, the General Assembly established an independent executive director with accompanying staff to represent customers in rate cases and other utilities matters. This "public" staff also supplies technical assistance to the Utilities Commission.

Department of Correction

The Department of Correction has two main divisions which both deal with persons convicted of crimes. The Division of Prisons supervises youths, men and women committed to active prison terms. The Division of Adult Probation and Parole is responsible for convicted offenders who have been given suspended sentences or who have served time in prison and are released on parole.

It is the responsibility of the Department of Correction, under the secretary of correction, to protect law-abiding citizens from those who have been convicted of crimes by providing appropriate custodial care of prisoners and by rehabilitating convicted offenders as much as possible with the resources provided by the state.

Some 16,400 persons were in North Carolina prisons as of March, 1982. At that time, there were 85 facilities in the correctional system ranging from the one maximum custody institution for men, Central Prison in Raleigh, to numerous minimum custody camps, advancement centers and halfway houses. The major institution for women, the North Carolina Correctional Center for Women, is also in Raleigh.

Eight facilities comprise the Youth Services Complex under the Division of Prisons. Youths, ages 16-21, who have been tried as adults for felony crimes, are housed in the eight facilities. Institutions for committed delinquent youths under 18 years of age are operated by the Department of Human Resources.

All levels of academic education as well as several vocational training programs are offered at many prisons. On-the-job training, work-release programs and study-release programs are available to some inmates.

Prison Enterprises operates some 18 different industries from license plate manufacturing to farming operations.

The Division of Adult Probation and Parole was supervising some 38,000 persons on probation and 8,000 on parole as of March, 1982. The Pre-release and Aftercare Program has centers located in Asheville, Greensboro, Greenville, Raleigh and Wilmington to prepare eligible inmates for their release. The division offers pre-trial and pre-sentence services at the request of the court.

Boards and commissions under the Department of Correction's jurisdiction are:

> Board of Corrections
> Inmate Grievance Commission
> State Inmate Labor Commission
> Area Inmate Labor Commissions (6)
> Parole Commission
> N.C. Department of Correction Prison
> Enterprises

Department of Crime Control and Public Safety

The Department of Crime Control and Public Safety (CCPS) was created in 1977 to oversee all state agencies providing law enforcement and emergency services. While most such agencies were moved into the department, a few remain in other departments, including the State Bureau of Investigation (SBI), the Capital Security Police, wildlife enforcement officers and highway weight inspectors.

In the area of state-level law enforcement, the Department of Crime Control and Public Safety is generally responsible for enforcing highway and alcohol laws.

The state Highway Patrol primarily enforces highway laws. Troopers have police power, however, and may support local law enforcement when directed.

The Division of Alcohol Law Enforcement oversees the sale, purchase, transportation, manufacture and possession of intoxicating liquors and controlled substances. Because the Alcohol Law Enforcement Division and Highway Patrol can be involved in drug law enforcement, the agencies' activities occasionally overlap with or suffer from lack of coordination with those of the SBI. The SBI, in the Department of Justice, was given the assignment of primary drug law enforcement by a governor.

Other crime control functions are more clearly divided between CCPS and the SBI. For example, the SBI has original jurisdiction in thefts of state government property and illegal acts by state government officials. The Bureau can enter any case it is invited into by other state and local agencies and can undertake special projects at the governor's request. CCPS has overall responsibility for criminal justice planning and coordination.

The Crime Commission Division prepares an annual plan for the state's criminal justice system and provides support for the Governor's Crime Commission. The commission recommends proposals for an effective criminal justice system and distributes funds from the federal Juvenile Justice and Delinquency Prevention Fund and other grant sources when available. It also coordinates the state's efforts in restitution, reparation and victim assistance programs.

The Division of the National Guard is directed by the adjutant general of North Carolina. The Guard serves a dual role: as a state military force, subject to the call of the governor, and as a federal reserve force, subject to the call of the President. It is the only military force under the control of the state for use in exercising its sovereignty.

The Emergency Management Division plans and coordinates governmental services within the state during times of local, state or national emergencies. The type of emergency and areas involved determine whether the state Emergency Operating Center, maintained in Raleigh, is activated. This underground "nerve center" is where the governor directs emergency services during times of disaster.

The Civil Air Patrol is a totally volunteer organization providing public services such as search and rescue of downed aircraft. It is partially funded through the department, although the department exercises no operational control over it.

Other departmental duties include assisting local governments in citizen crime prevention activities and providing police and fire services for state installations at Butner and the surrounding town.

Some boards and commissions within the department's jurisdiction are:

> State Fire Commission
> Military Aides Commission
> Criminal Justice Information System
> Crime Prevention and Public Information Committee

Department of Cultural Resources

In 1971 the General Assembly established the Department of Cultural Resources—the first of its kind in any state. Its purpose is to promote and provide libraries and cultural resources, services and programs in the arts, history and other areas that enhance and enrich the lives of North Carolina citizens. The secretary oversees administration of the department's three divisions and special programs and serves on some boards.

The Division of Archives and History is responsible for the N.C. Museum of History in Raleigh, Tryon Palace in New Bern, historical publications, archives and records, state historical sites, archaeological and historic preservation and the

Tryon Palace—New Bern

Capitol Visitors' Services. The division identifies and preserves historical documents and records, artifacts, historical
properties and archaeological sites (underwater as well as
on land). Through its museums and historic sites, the division collects, refurbishes and displays countless items from
the state's past. It also produces scholarly and historical
publications.

The Historic Sites Section publishes a list of the state's
historic sites. It is available free from the Department of
Cultural Resources (address in Appendix A).

The Division of the Arts also operates a museum—the
N.C. Museum of Art in Raleigh. A special feature of the
museum is a gallery for the blind, which approaches explora-
tion of art through touch.

In addition to developing and preserving art collections,
the Division of the Arts supports art exhibits and performing
arts groups through the N.C. Arts Council. The council helps
bring artists into schools and communities across the state to
support the development of the arts at the local level.

A theater section of the Division of the Arts was created to
help upgrade the professional level of existing theater groups.
Emphasis has been on support to outdoor dramas and other
non-profit professional theater companies.

The division also provides some administrative services to
the North Carolina Symphony.

The Division of the State Library furnishes technical and
informational aids and establishes services to state agencies
and local public libraries. Special libraries for the blind and
collections in state institutions are established and maintained by this division. The Technical Services Section operates a processing center for libraries in the state, which makes
it possible for local libraries to get books easily and at less
expense.

A recent addition to the Department of Cultural Resources
is the Office of Folklife Programs, which helps identify and
preserve traditional arts and skills.

Some of the more than 30 boards and commissions under
the department's jurisdiction are:

Public Library Certification Commission
Historic Bath Commission

Executive Mansion Fine Arts Committee
Edenton Historical Commission
U.S.S. North Carolina Battleship Commission
Archaeological Advisory Committee
Abandoned Cemeteries Commission
Roanoke Island Association

Department of Human Resources

The Department of Human Resources is one of the largest state agencies with a wide variety of services and programs under its administration, such as mental health, waste management, welfare and juvenile detention facilities. The department is responsible for developing policies and managing state and federal programs that will help all citizens achieve and maintain an adequate level of health and social and economic well-being. The Board of Human Resources acts as an advisory body to the secretary regarding human services programs. The board is composed of the chairmen of the five commissions within the department and nine members at large, appointed by the governor. The secretary serves ex officio as chairman.

Most of the human services—welfare, health care and rehabilitation—are actually delivered in the state by local human services agencies, such as mental health centers and health and social services departments. The Department of Human Resources establishes and enforces the standards for these services. Other services are delivered directly through field staff and institutions located throughout the state. Four regional offices at Asheville, Winston-Salem, Fayetteville and Greenville serve as an extension to the department's management staff and provide supervision and consultation to the field staff.

North Carolina has a state-supervised/county-administered social services system. The Department of Human Resources Division of Social Services supervises the administration of the federal government's Aid to Families with Dependent Children and food stamps, the state/county general assistance program and social services programs administered by the county departments. The division has four main service sections: child support enforcement, family services, income maintenance and disability determination. An 11-member Social Services Commission establishes policy for this program.

The Division of Mental Health, Mental Retardation and Substance Abuse Services provides services to eligible people through a system of state-operated institutions and locally-operated community mental health programs. Residential care and treatment are offered at four regional psychiatric hospitals, four mental retardation centers, three alcoholic rehabilitation centers and a re-education program for emotionally disturbed children. A major thrust of this division is community-based services. A wide variety of programs, such as sheltered workshops, day activity programs and halfway houses, are being developed to allow eligible patients to live and/or work outside of large institutions. The N.C. Commission for Mental Health, Mental Retardation and Substance Abuse Services establishes rules and regulations for the programs.

The Division of Health Services serves public health needs by providing consulting services to county and local health departments in numerous areas, including environmental health. In addition, the division operates special care centers: regional clinics for crippled children, the Lenox Baker Cerebral Palsy and Crippled Children's Hospital in Durham, Orthopedic Hospital in Gastonia and McCain Hospital in McCain for treatment of tuberculosis and other chest diseases.

The Division of Medical Assistance has full responsibility for the state's Medicaid programs, including establishing policy, determining eligibility, analyzing financial status and needs and monitoring.

The Division of Vocational Rehabilitation Services is responsible for the federal/state program to help those with a mental or physical disability join the work force.

The Division of Youth Services develops and supervises the state institutions for committed delinquent children, putting emphasis on treatment and therapy, community-based programs, alternatives to institutionalization and preventative measures. The five schools are in Eagle Springs, Kinston, Concord, Swannanoa and Butner.

Department of

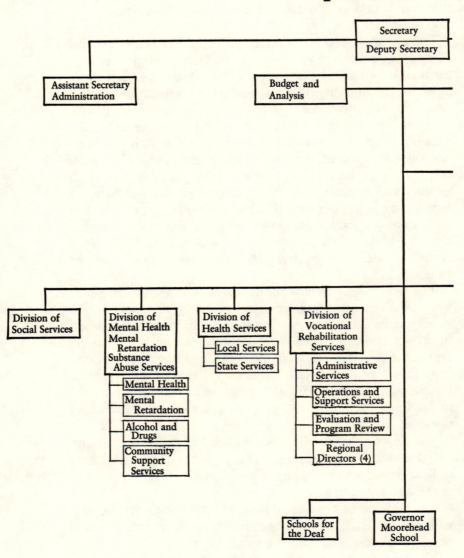

Secretary

Deputy Secretary

Assistant Secretary
Administration

Budget and
Analysis

Division of
Social Services

Division of
Mental Health
Mental
　Retardation
Substance
　Abuse Services

- Mental Health
- Mental
　Retardation
- Alcohol and
　Drugs
- Community
　Support
　Services

Division of
Health Services

- Local Services
- State Services

Division of
Vocational
Rehabilitation
Services

Administrative
Services

Operations and
Support Services

Evaluation and
Program Review

Regional
Directors (4)

Schools for
the Deaf

Governor
Moorehead
School

Human Resources

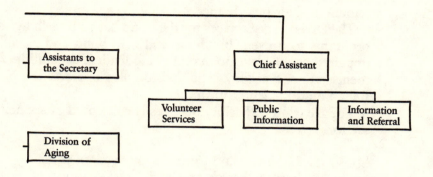

- Assistants to the Secretary
- Chief Assistant
  - Volunteer Services
  - Public Information
  - Information and Referral
- Division of Aging

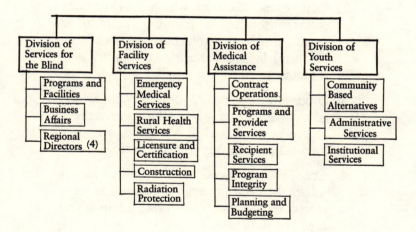

- Division of Services for the Blind
  - Programs and Facilities
  - Business Affairs
  - Regional Directors (4)
- Division of Facility Services
  - Emergency Medical Services
  - Rural Health Services
  - Licensure and Certification
  - Construction
  - Radiation Protection
- Division of Medical Assistance
  - Contract Operations
  - Programs and Provider Services
  - Recipient Services
  - Program Integrity
  - Planning and Budgeting
- Division of Youth Services
  - Community Based Alternatives
  - Administrative Services
  - Institutional Services

The Division of Aging is establishing focal points in all 100 counties for one-stop comprehensive services along with increased health and nutrition services to help senior citizens remain in their own homes.

The Division of Services for the Blind has responsibility for programs to prevent blindness and help blind and visually-impaired people develop maximum individual capabilities for themselves and society. The division also operates the N.C. Rehabilitation Center in Butner.

The Division of Facility Services is composed of six major sections:

1. Licensure and Certification Section, which licenses health and social services institutions, radiation facilities and organizations which solicit funds. It also inspects local jails and other confinement facilities.

2. Construction Section, which provides consultation services for planning, building or remodeling health and social services facilities and inspects facilities for safety and function.

3. Office of Emergency Medical Services, which administers programs for the improvement of pre-hospital and in-hospital emergency medical care throughout the state.

4. Certificate of Need Section, which determines the need for new or additional medical care facilities or equipment in given areas of the state.

5. Radiation Protection Section, which has direct jurisdiction over the possession, transfer, disposal and use of ionizing radiation sources.

6. Rural Health Section, which has been establishing rural health centers in medically deprived areas in an attempt to provide accessible care to rural citizens.

It also operates a statewide physician recruitment program.

The N.C. Medical Care Commission sets policy for several of the division's programs, including health facility construction grants and loans, licensing standards for hospitals, criteria for certifying emergency medical technicians and regulations for certifying ambulances.

Schools for the deaf and blind—for children 6-18 years of age—also are administered by the Department of Human Resources. The Governor Morehead School in Raleigh is the residential school for the blind. Three residential schools serve deaf children in Morganton, Wilson and Greensboro. This division also coordinates a community education program for the deaf through the community college system.

The department has become, through its Radiation Protection and Health Services Commissions, the main agency for waste management in North Carolina. It has the primary regulatory authority for hazardous waste in the state, administers the solid waste and hazardous waste acts, establishes and enforces regulations for all phases of waste management, including collection, transportation, storage, treatment and disposal and has responsibility for issuing permits for hazardous waste facilities.

Some of the other boards under the jurisdiction of the department are:

Council on Developmental Disabilities
N.C. Drug Commission
Council on Sickle Cell Syndrome
State Board of Examiners for Nursing Home
    Administrators
Governor's Council on Physical Fitness and
    Health
N.C. Water Treatment Facility Operators
    Certification Board
Statewide Perinatal Advisory Council
Governor's Waste Management Board

Department of Natural Resources and Community Development

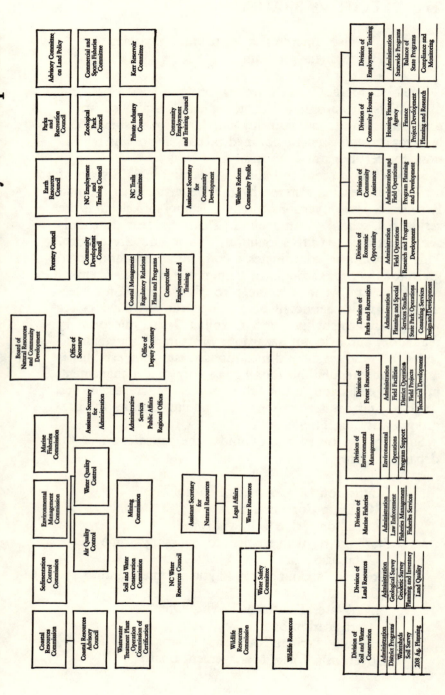

Regional Offices Asheville Fayetteville Mooresville Raleigh Washington Wilmington Winston-Salem

THE EXECUTIVE BRANCH

Department of Natural Resources and Community Development

Primary goals of the Department of Natural Resources and Community Development are to protect and manage natural resources and to promote orderly development of the state's communities. These goals include increasing the ability of communities to plan for accommodating development and the people accompanying that development. Responsibilities of various offices in the department range from air quality control to the state zoo.

Services offered to citizens through the department's field offices are community and land use planning, economic development, water and air protection and recreation assistance. The field offices are located in Asheville, Mooresville, Winston-Salem, Wilmington, Fayetteville, Raleigh and Washington.

The secretary, the deputy secretary and the assistant secretaries have primary responsibility for guiding development of the N.C. Zoological Park near Asheboro, operating coastal zone management and wood energy programs, providing environmental assessments and administering federal grants-in-aid programs. The wood energy program is operated cooperatively with the Department of Commerce.

Community development functions of the department are carried out by the Divisions of Community Assistance, State Economic Opportunity, Community Housing and Employment and Training. The department administers state operations of the Comprehensive Employment and Training Act (CETA).

Functions of the department in the area of natural resources are handled by the Office of Water Resources and the Divisions of Environmental Management, Forest Resources, Land Resources, Soil and Water Conservation, Marine Fisheries and Parks and Recreation.

The Wildlife Resources Commission manages the wildlife resources of North Carolina and administers the laws related to game, freshwater fish and other wildlife resources. An Interagency Wildlife Coordination Section monitors and coordinates activities of other agencies that impact upon fish and wildlife to ameliorate their adverse effects.

67

The Boating Division conducts boating and water safety programs of the agency, including the development and maintenance of 130 access areas to public waters throughout the state.

Some of the numerous boards and commissions under the department's jurisdiction are:

> Board of Natural Resources and Community Development
> N.C. Employment and Training Council
> N.C. Forestry Council
> Forest Fire Protection Commission
> N.C. Mining Commission
> N.C. Sedimentation Control Commission
> Soil and Water Conservation Commission
> N.C. Coastal Resources Commission
> N.C. Environmental Management Commission
> N.C. Marine Fisheries Commission
> Parks and Recreation Council

Department of Revenue

The Department of Revenue administers North Carolina tax laws and regulations. It is taxpayers who provide the money to operate state government. The Department of Revenue collects the taxes from individuals and businesses. And the state treasurer acts as the "banker" or custodian of the money until it is disbursed by state departments and agencies in accordance with a budget approved by the General Assembly.

The department is divided into two broad areas: tax schedule administration and administrative services. The seven divisions which administer tax schedules are:

1. Inheritance and gift tax
2. Individual income tax
3. Corporate income and franchise tax
4. Gasoline tax
5. Intangibles tax

6. Sales and use tax

7. Privilege licenses and beverage and
   cigarette taxes

In addition to handling state taxes, the department also collects the one percent local sales tax and distributes the proceeds to local governments. Portions of "shared" taxes are also distributed to local governments, including the beer and wine excise taxes, intangible personal property taxes and certain franchise taxes.

In the area of administrative services, the Ad Valorem Tax Division assists local governments in the administration of local property taxes, including the valuation and taxation of real and personal property. The staff of this division also serves the Property Tax Commission which hears cases where property valuations are contested by property owners.

Another administrative service is the Tax Research Division. This division compiles statistical data on state and local taxation, publishes a biennial report and prepares estimates of revenue and the effects of proposed changes in revenue laws and of new sources of revenue.

The secretary of revenue serves as chairman of the Property Tax Commission.

Department of Transportation

The Department of Transportation is responsible for providing services and facilities to meet the present and future transportation and highway safety needs of North Carolina. The secretary of transportation is ex officio chairman of the Board of Transportation, which oversees transportation policy and development in the state. The board is composed of 23 other members—21 appointed by the governor, one by the lieutenant governor and one by the speaker of the House.

The Division of Highways is in charge of constructing, maintaining and operating the statewide network of roads, streets, highways, interstates and ferries as determined by the Board of Transportation. (In North Carolina, all county roads are part of the state highway system.) The division uses both state and federal funds in its highway improvement program.

Cape Hatteras Lighthouse

THE EXECUTIVE BRANCH

The Division of Motor Vehicles regulates ownership and operation of motor vehicles and enforces the laws applying to drivers and vehicles, including licensing drivers, registering vehicles, administering the safety inspection and driver safety education programs, and carrying out the weight control and theft tracing program.

The development of a safe and efficient system of airports and air ways is the responsibility of the Division of Aviation. The division works, with policy direction from the Aeronautics Council, to expand air commerce, improve airports through grants and technical assistance, increase air transportation services in the state and promote aviation safety.

The Division of Public Transportation provides grants and technical assistance to local governments for the improvement of both urban and rural public transit systems. Programs include providing assistance in the coordination of human services transportation, providing technical assistance and promotion for ridesharing efforts of all kinds—carpooling, vanpooling and buspooling—and providing technical assistance to the intercity bus industry. The division operates under the guidance of the Public Transportation Advisory Council.

The department's bicycle program provides education and enforcement advisory services and facility technical assistance for local bicycle programs, operating through a statewide Bicycle Committee.

The state rail program provides limited grants and technical assistance to the short and branch lines in the state in need of rehabilitation. North Carolina is the majority stockholder of the North Carolina Railroad and the Atlantic and North Carolina Railroad. These two companies own the entire rail right of way from Morehead City to Charlotte, via Goldsboro, Raleigh and the Piedmont Crescent. The right of way is leased to Southern Railway.

Department of Community Colleges

The Department of Community Colleges is technically an executive department, but operates completely independently from the governor's office. The department is discussed in detail in Chapter V on Higher Education.

THE PRESENT COURT SYSTEM
Original Jurisdiction and Routes of Appeal

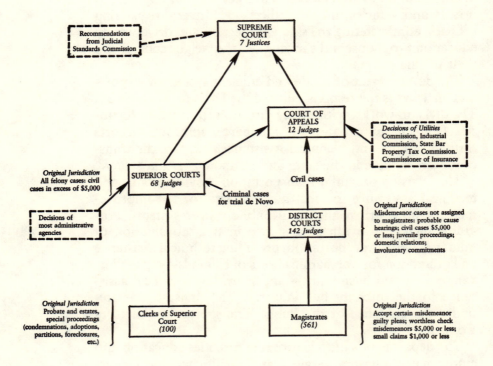

(1) Appeals from the Court of Appeals to the Supreme Court are by right in Utilities Commission general rate cases, cases involving constitutional questions, and cases in which there has been dissent in the Court of Appeals. In its discretion, the Supreme Court may review Court of Appeals decisions in cases of significant public interest or cases involving legal principles of major significance.

(2) Appeals from these agencies lie directly to the Court of Appeals.

(3) As a matter of right, appeals go directly to the Supreme Court in criminal cases in which the defendant has been sentenced to death or life imprisonment, and in civil cases involving the involuntary annexation of territory by a municipality of 5,000 or more population. In all other cases appeal as of right is to the Court of Appeals. In its discretion, the Supreme Court may hear appeals directly from the trial courts in cases where delay would cause substantial harm or the Court of Appeals docket is unusually full.

**Information provided by NC Administrative Office of the Courts.

CHAPTER IV.

THE JUDICIAL BRANCH

Court reform efforts in the 1950s resulted in constitutional amendments, passed in 1962, establishing a unified court system. The numerous courts operated by various levels of government were combined into a General Court of Justice for the purposes of jurisdiction, operation and administration. The system includes three divisions: the Appellate Division, the Superior Court Division and the District Court Division. The Appellate Division has two branches—the Court of Appeals and the Supreme Court.

In 1965 the General Assembly enacted statutes to put the system into effect by stages. By the end of 1970 all of the counties and their courts had been incorporated into the new system.[1] There are now no locally-funded or locally-controlled trial courts in any county.

The Supreme Court

The Supreme Court has a chief justice and six associate justices who are elected for terms of eight years. The court decides questions of law presented in civil and criminal cases, including constitutional questions, appealed from lower courts. It does not hear witnesses or have juries.

While most cases go to the Supreme Court through the Court of Appeals, some cases are appealed directly to the Supreme Court. These are cases from the Utilities Commission, convictions of felony offenses in which the death sentence or life imprisonment was imposed and involuntary annexations of territory by a municipality. The court can also

---

1. Administrative Office of the Courts, *North Carolina Courts, 1979-80, Annual Report* (Raleigh: Administrative Office of the Courts, January, 1981), p. 8.

choose to bypass the Court of Appeals and hear an appeal directly from a lower court, at its own discretion.

The only original jurisdiction the Supreme Court has is in deciding upon censure and removal of judges, after hearing recommendations of the Judicial Standards Commission. All sessions of the court are in Raleigh.

The General Assembly gave the Supreme Court the power to supervise and control the proceedings of the other courts of the General Court of Justice, such as prescribing rules of practice and procedures and approving the superior courts' schedules of sessions. The chief justice appoints the director of the Administrative Office of the Courts. That agency is responsible for direction of the non-judicial, administrative and business affairs of the judicial department.

The Court of Appeals

Twelve judges, elected for terms of eight years, serve on the Court of Appeals. The court sits in panels of three judges each to hear and decide cases. It usually sits in Raleigh but may be authorized by the Supreme Court to hold court in other places throughout the state.

This court considers and decides cases appealed from district and superior courts. It also hears appeals directly from the Industrial Commission and from certain final orders or decisions of the State Bar Association, the commissioner of insurance and the Property Tax Commission. Like the Supreme Court, the Court of Appeals does not have juries or hear witnesses. Decisions of this court may be appealed to the Supreme Court.

The Superior Courts

The superior court is the major trial court in North Carolina. It has original jurisdiction in all felony cases (major crimes) and in civil cases in which the amount in controversy exceeds $5,000. Misdemeanor convictions in the district court may be appealed to the superior court for a new trial before a jury. Appeals from all administrative agencies, except those specifically designated to be heard by the Court of Appeals and the Supreme Court, are taken to the superior court, as are appeals of rulings made by the clerk of superior court.

Each county of the state has a superior court session at least twice a year, lasting a minimum of one week each. Most of the counties have much more than the constitutional minimum number of sessions, and several have one or more superior courts in session almost every week of the year.

The state is divided into 34 judicial districts, comprised of one or more counties, with the most populous counties making up a single-county district. The districts are grouped into four divisions within which a superior court judge must rotate from one district to the next. Each of the districts has at least one superior court judge as a resident. There are a total of 60 superior court judges, each elected for an eight-year term. Eight additional special superior court judges are appointed by the governor for terms of four years. The special judges are assigned by the chief justice of the Supreme Court to serve in any county where they may be needed.

The District Courts

District court also is held in each of the 100 counties of the state. This court has jurisdiction to try misdemeanor cases, civil cases in which the amount in controversy is $5,000 or less, domestic relations cases and juvenile cases. These courts handle a much greater volume of cases than do the superior courts.

There were some 142 district court judges in 1982 allocated among the 34 judicial districts, ranging from two judges in the least populated districts to nine judges in the most populated district (Mecklenburg County). The chief justice of the Supreme Court appoints a chief district judge in each district who is responsible for scheduling district court sessions. District court judges are elected for four-year terms.

In addition to the district court judges, there are 561 magistrates in the District Court Division. They may hear and decide small claims cases ($1,000 or less) and accept guilty pleas in certain misdemeanor cases. In addition, a great part of the magistrate workload is in issuing arrest warrants in hearings for probable cause in misdemeanor or felony cases. Magistrates in each county are appointed by the senior

75

MAP OF JUDICIAL DISTRICTS

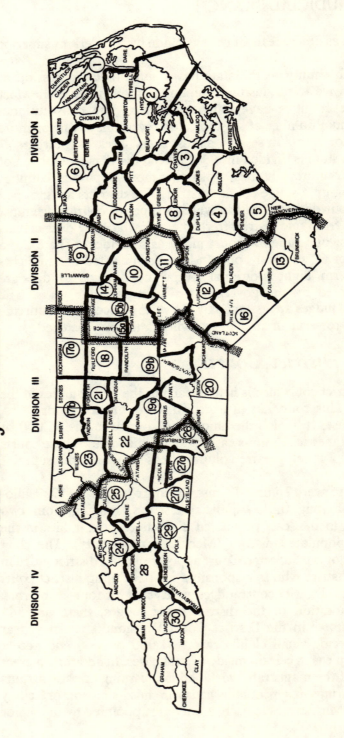

DIVISION I

DIVISION II

DIVISION III

DIVISION IV

resident superior court judge upon recommendation of the clerk of the superior court. The chief district court judge supervises magistrates in carrying out their duties.

District Attorney

The principal duty of the district attorney is to prosecute all criminal cases, felony and misdemeanor, in both the district and superior courts. Each district attorney is authorized to employ a certain number of assistant district attorneys, ranging from two in the least populated districts to 19 in the largest district. District attorneys are elected for four-year terms from prosecutorial districts, which coincide with the 34 judicial districts.

Clerk of the Superior Court

Each of the 100 counties has a clerk of the superior court, elected for a four-year term. The clerk is responsible for all clerical and record-keeping functions in both the superior and district courts in the county. In addition, the clerk serves as ex officio judge of probate (settlement of estates) and acts as the initial judge in such special proceedings as adoptions, condemnations of private property under the public's right of eminent domain and foreclosures. The clerk also is empowered to issue search and arrest warrants and subpoenas. The clerk may accept guilty pleas in certain misdemeanor offenses and impose fines in accordance with a schedule established by district court judges.

Public Defender

Six judicial districts have been designated by the General Assembly to have full-time public defenders to provide legal representation for persons charged with serious crimes who are determined to be indigent. In the other 28 districts, private counsel is assigned to those eligible.

Five of the public defenders are appointed by the governor for four-year terms from recommendations submitted by the respective district bar associations (Districts 3, 12, 18, 26 and 27A). In District 28 the appointment is made by the senior resident superior court judge.

The Trial Jury

A trial jury is a group of people sworn to hear evidence about a case, as presented in court, and make a decision in accordance with its findings. In criminal cases tried in superior court, twelve persons must serve on each jury, and the verdict must be unanimous to convict. Twelve persons also serve on each jury for civil cases, unless the parties agree to have fewer jurors or even waive jury trial and have the case heard and decided by the presiding judge. The parties in a civil case also may agree to have the case decided by a majority rather than unanimous verdict of the jury.

Jurors select a foreman from among themselves when deliberations begin.

Tax rolls, voter registration rosters and driver's license lists comprise the lists from which jurors may be selected at random. No occupation or class of person is automatically excused from reporting for jury duty, although persons over 65 must be excused upon request. A few counties have adopted a system of calling jurors for one day or one trial, whichever is longer, instead of requiring a juror's presence for an entire week or term of court.

The Grand Jury

A grand jury has several functions, but principally decides whether or not there seems to be enough evidence to proceed with a trial of a person accused of a crime. In order to be charged with a felony, a defendant must be served a "true bill of indictment." When a defendant has been bound over for trial in superior court, the prosecutor must submit to the grand jury a bill of indictment stating the charges. The grand jury hears and questions witnesses called by the prosecutor— and may request others, then decides whether it is a "true bill of indictment" or "not a true bill of indictment." A jury foreman selected by the judge presides over all proceedings, which are secret.

The grand jury proceeding differs from a probable cause hearing, which is conducted first, in that a judge presides over the probable cause hearing and lawyers may be present and use it as a chance for discovery. In addition, the probable cause hearing is not a guaranteed process.

Grand juries may also issue presentments, or results of investigations initiated on their own or requested by a judge or prosecutor, although this is rarely done in North Carolina. The grand jury also has the duty to inspect the jail and may inspect other county offices or agencies.

A total of 18 persons are selected for a grand jury to serve an entire year, meeting at regular intervals or when needed. (Certain large districts have two grand juries serving concurrently, meeting on alternate Mondays, to spread the workload.) The finding on an indictment, the return of a presentment or any other decision of a grand jury requires concurrence of at least 12 members.

Organizational Chart
The University of
North Carolina System

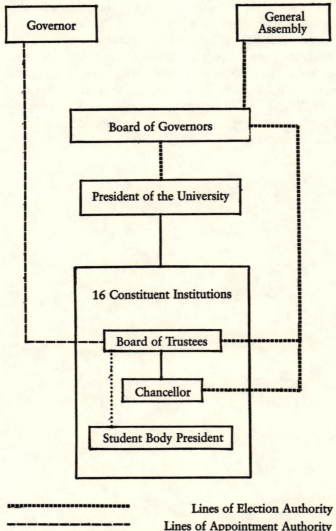

	Lines of Election Authority
	Lines of Appointment Authority
	Lines of Ex-Officio Membership
	Lines of Direct Authority

CHAPTER V

HIGHER EDUCATION

The University of North Carolina

Sixteen colleges and universities comprise the University of North Carolina. The University of North Carolina at Chapel Hill was chartered in 1789 and opened in 1795. In 1931, the first of several mergers of public institutions of higher education took place, starting the multicampus system of the University of North Carolina. In 1972, all 16 four-year state-supported colleges and universities in the state were consolidated into the system.

The 16 institutions fall into five general categories:

Major Research Universities

> University of North Carolina at Chapel Hill
> North Carolina State University (Raleigh)

Other Doctoral-granting University

> University of North Carolina at Greensboro

Comprehensive Universities

> Appalachian State University (Boone)
> East Carolina University (Greenville)
> North Carolina Agricultural and Technical
>   State University (Greensboro)
> North Carolina Central University (Durham)
> University of North Carolina at Charlotte
> Western Carolina University (Cullowhee)

General Baccalaureate Universities with Limited Master's Work

> Elizabeth City State University
> Fayetteville State University
> Pembroke State University
> University of North Carolina at Asheville
> University of North Carolina at Wilmington
> Winston-Salem State University

Specialized Institution

> North Carolina School of the Arts (Winston-Salem)

Medical schools have been established at UNC-Chapel Hill and East Carolina. N.C. Central University and UNC-Chapel Hill have law schools.

A 32-member Board of Governors chosen by the legislature governs the university system. The board names the university president who has responsibility for university-wide administration and execution of board policy. The board also is responsible for N.C. Memorial Hospital, the Agricultural Research Service and the Agricultural Extension Service.

Each constituent institution has a 13-member board of trustees. Eight members are named by the Board of Governors, four are appointed by the governor, and the student body president serves ex officio.

The Board of Governors decides most financial matters for the university, such as budget, tuition and student fees at each institution. It also makes the final decision on such things as campus construction, organization of academic departments and appointments of faculty members with tenure.

Each board of trustees primarily serves as an adviser to the chancellor and Board of Governors concerning the management and development of the institution. Within university and legislative guidelines, the board of trustees does have the authority to decide such things as personnel policies, criteria for admissions, participation in intercollegiate athletics, rules for student aid programs and kinds of student services to be offered, among others.

The Institute of Government is a part of UNC-Chapel Hill and is devoted to research, teaching and consultation in state and local government. The Institute's Legislative Reporting Service records and reports daily activities of the General Assembly. In addition, the Institute serves as a research agency for numerous study commissions of state and local governments.

The North Carolina Agricultural Extension Service is a cooperative effort of N.C. Agricultural and Technical State University, N.C. State University and the U.S. Department of Agriculture. The service operates a county office in each of the 100 N.C. counties. The state and county offices disseminate information acquired through research performed at the nation's agricultural and technical universities. The service prepares publications on thousands of topics such as canning, energy efficiency, land management and farming techniques and offers a wide variety of classes and programs to citizens, primarily in rural communities. The Extension Service also operates Teletip, at a toll free telephone number listed in Appendix A, on which a citizen may request and listen to a taped message, based on an Extension Service publication. A catalog of available tapes may be ordered from the Agricultural Extension Service, N.C. State University, Raleigh, N.C. 27607.

The University Television Network is owned by the statewide university and is operated as a public service to provide television programs for educational purposes, information dissemination and cultural enrichment. In 1979 the UNC Center for Public Television was established to coordinate and improve public television.

Some 118,761 students were enrolled in the University of North Carolina during the 1981-82 school year.

There are also some 30 private senior colleges and universities in North Carolina, eight private two-year institutions and four Bible colleges and theological seminaries. North Carolina students at these private schools receive state assistance, amounting to as much as $800 per student in the 1981-82 academic year. A $600 payment was made to a school for each North Carolina student enrolled, and an additional

83

$200 was paid as a scholarship for each needy North Carolina student. Much larger payments are made for each North Carolina student enrolled in the Duke University and Wake Forest University medical schools.

Community Colleges

A half million students enroll each year in the 58 institutions comprising the North Carolina community college system. Originally, these institutions were placed under the State Board of Education. However, in 1979 the General Assembly consolidated administration of all state technical institutes, technical colleges and community colleges in the State Department of Community Colleges. It was established as a separate entity in the executive branch (G.S. 115D).

The Department of Community Colleges does not resemble other executive departments in that it operates quite independently of the governor. The governor does not appoint the head of the department, and that person does not meet and consult with the governor's cabinet or executive cabinet.

The Community College system is governed by the State Board of Community Colleges. Its 19 members are appointed to six-year terms. The governor appoints 10 members; the General Assembly elects seven members; and the state treasurer and lieutenant governor are ex officio members. The president of the system is elected by the board.

Community colleges fill the gap in educational opportunity between high school and the senior colleges and universities for high school graduates and those who are beyond the compulsory age limit of the public schools. The major purpose of each school is to offer vocational and technical education and training and the necessary academic education needed to profit from the job training. The technical institutes and colleges and community colleges offer different levels of academic, cultural and occupational education, ranging from basic education through the two-year college level. The programs and services offered by each institution are designed to reflect the needs and concerns of the citizens and industries in the community served. Nearly three-fourths of all students enroll in job training programs.

The Old Well
UNC–Chapel Hill

CHAPTER VI.

FINANCING STATE GOVERNMENT

Services rendered by the state to its citizens must be paid for primarily by those same citizens. As the population of the state has grown, the complexity of government has increased, and, therefore, its cost. When North Carolina was a colony owned by the Lords Proprietors and later by the King of England, taxes were levied to make it a profitable venture. In 1977, voters approved a constitutional amendment requiring the state to adopt a balanced budget. This process actually had been in practice since the 1925 Executive Budget Act. The Constitution also requires the governor to monitor revenue collection throughout the year and "effect the necessary economies in state expenditures" to insure that the state does not incur a deficit.[1]

Budgets

Budget-making is the process by which governments match their anticipated financial resources to necessary and desirable services. The budget is not only a source of financial information about money received and disbursed, it is also an accounting of the services provided to the state's citizens. As the *Handbook for Legislators* points out, "The General Assembly can most effectively direct state government by

---

1. *Constitution of the State of North Carolina* (as of July, 1980), Article III, Sec. 5(3).

STATE OF NORTH CAROLINA
REVENUES AND EXPENDITURES
FOR THE FISCAL YEAR ENDING

JUNE 30, 1981

REVENUES

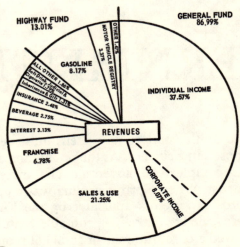

GENERAL FUND:

Income:		
Individual	$1,303,517,221	
Corporation	279,803,897	$1,583,321,118
Sales and Use		737,098,123
Franchise		235,280,325
Interest		108,546,785
Beverage		95,389,760
Insurance		86,188,075
Inheritance and Gift		45,603,096
Soft Drink		22,278,966
Judicial Department Receipts		21,430,978
Cigarette		18,247,220
License		13,593,971
Building and Loan		8,299,643
Other		42,609,922[a]
Total General Fund		$3,017,887,982[b]

HIGHWAY FUND:

Gasoline	$ 283,528,482	
Motor Vehicle Registration	117,039,613	
Interest and Miscellaneous Revenue	39,128,122[c]	
Gasoline Inspection Fees	8,108,561	
Property Owners, Cities and Towns Participation	3,491,576	
Total Highway Fund		$ 451,296,354[d]
TOTAL REVENUES		$3,469,184,336

NOTES: Revenues do not include (1) Federal Aid other than General Shared Federal Revenue, (2) receipts of special funds, (3) institutional earnings, (4) proceeds from sale, lease, or rental of State property, and (5) agricultural fees and receipts.

[a]Includes General Shared Federal Revenue amounting to $28,391,897.
[b]Excludes reversions of capital improvement appropriations amounting to $4,950,481.
[c]Includes $12,700,000 in Contracting Authorization.
[d]Excludes (1) $4,940,000 transferred from General Fund, (2) $1,636,347 in Grants and General Participation, (3) $209,129,349 in Federal Aid, and (4) Transfer of $66,437 to Comprehensive Employment and Training Act.

STATE OF NORTH CAROLINA
REVENUES AND EXPENDITURES
FOR THE FISCAL YEAR ENDING

JUNE 30, 1981
EXPENDITURES

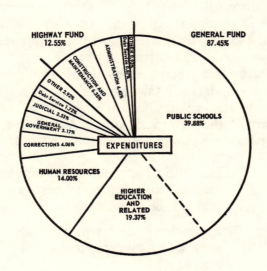

GENERAL FUND:

Education		
Public Schools	$1,390,907,313	
Higher Education	653,120,138	
Related Education Activities*	22,400,192	$2,066,427,643
Human Resources		488,201,903
Corrections		141,575,912
General Government		110,691,872
Judicial		81,229,801
Debt Service		60,044,412
Resource Development and Preservation		36,949,742
Public Safety and Regulation		36,633,690
Agriculture		19,836,531
Legislative		8,421,402
Total General Fund		$3,050,012,908**

HIGHWAY FUND:		
Construction and Maintenance	$ 221,513,711	
Administration	153,390,267	
State Aid to Municipalities	32,522,000	
Debt Service	30,329,757	
Total Highway Fund		$ 437,755,735
TOTAL EXPENDITURES		$3,487,768,643

NOTES: Expenditures from special funds, from institutional earnings, from Federal Aid and for permanent
improvements other than roads are excluded. Highway expenditures from Federal Aid amounted to
$174,280,201.

   *Includes expenditures of $18,589,277 for operation of the Department of Cultural Resources and
expenditures of $3,810,915 for the North Carolina School of the Arts.
   **Excludes $104,141,290 for capital improvements.

N. C. DEPARTMENT OF REVENUE TAX RESEARCH DIVISION

deciding what part of the state's revenue is to be used for what purposes."[2]

According to the Constitution, it is the governor who submits a budget to the legislature for its consideration and administers the budget the General Assembly approves. But state law mandates that the Advisory Budget Commission (G.S. 143-4) participates in the budget preparation and also advises in the administration of it.

The budget process begins almost 18 months ahead of the time the budget will take effect. Requests from state agencies are submitted to the Office of State Budget and Management, a part of the governor's office. Anticipated needs of state agencies are separated into three categories:

1. Base budget or continuation budget, which includes expenditures for existing programs that will be continued.

2. Expansion budget, which includes enlargement of existing programs and new programs.

3. Capital expenditures, which includes construction, repairs and remodeling.

The Office of State Budget and Management and the governor review the requests (except for the budgets of the state auditor and state treasurer) and determine a total budget to recommend to the Advisory Budget Commission. "The likely influence of this group can be seen from its composition," according to the *Handbook for Legislators*.[3] Four of the 12 commission members are the chairmen of the Senate and House Appropriations and Finance Committees, two are appointed by the president of the Senate and two are appointed by the speaker of the House. The other four are appointed by the governor, "and they are often legislators or

---

2. Michael Crowell and Milton S. Heath, Jr., *The General Assembly of North Carolina, A Handbook for Legislators* (fourth edition), (Chapel Hill: Institute of Government, 1981), p. 82.

3. Crowell and Heath, p. 83.

former legislators."[4] The commission holds public hearings and closed deliberations, then adopts its final recommendations for the governor to submit to the General Assembly. If the governor and the Advisory Budget Commission disagree, the governor sends his proposal to the legislature and includes in it the commission's minority report.

Final decisions about the budget are made by the General Assembly after lengthy deliberations in appropriations committees. Traditionally, the appropriations subcommittees of the House and Senate meet jointly for their deliberations. Assistance in the work is provided not only by the state budget office but also by the General Assembly's own Division of Fiscal Research. Since so many legislators are involved in the appropriations committee process, the budget proposals generally provoke little debate on the floor prior to approval.

The General Assembly passes a biennial budget in a regular session. It then is reviewed and may be revised in a short budgetary session during the interim year. The state's fiscal year runs from July 1 to June 30.

The Advisory Budget Commission's additional power is in its statutory authority to advise the governor, as revenue collections are monitored, in the determinations of how much of the funds appropriated by the General Assembly should actually be allocated to spend. Commission members also constitute the State Board of Awards, which advises the governor on purchase contracts to be approved.

Taxes

Money to pay for the governmental appropriations, as decided by the General Assembly, comes from taxation. The state budget office estimates the amount of revenue anticipated for the biennium. The General Assembly then bases its spending decisions on the amount of revenue expected during those years.

The individual income tax has been providing more than one-third of the total tax revenue in recent years. Brackets of

4. *Ibid.*

ESTIMATED TOTAL STATE EXPENDITURES, 1982–83
BY SOURCE OF FUNDS

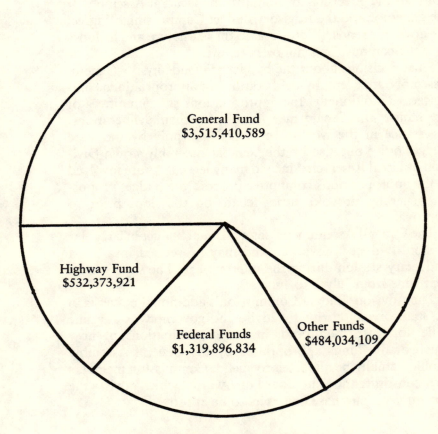

General Fund
$3,515,410,589

Highway Fund
$532,373,921

Federal Funds
$1,319,896,834

Other Funds
$484,034,109

1982–83 Total: $5,851,715,453

net taxable income of individuals are taxed in the range of three to seven percent. Corporations pay a six percent income tax. The state government levies a three percent sales tax on most items, including food. Motor vehicles, boats, etc. are taxed at two percent; farm and manufacturing machinery are taxed at one percent. Counties may, at their option, apply an additional one percent tax on sales subject to the three percent rate.

Receipts from the 12 cents-per-gallon gasoline tax (plus the 1/4 cent per gallon inspection fee) and from motor vehicle registrations are kept in a separate highway fund. One cent of the gasoline tax is returned to municipalities for maintenance of city streets.

Other taxes and fees North Carolina collects include the following: occupational license fees, intangibles tax, cigarette tax, soft drink tax, alcoholic beverages tax, inheritance tax, franchise tax and gift tax. Some of these are shared with local governments. In addition, there are local taxes as set by the cities and counties, most notably the property tax. Corporations pay a charter or entrance tax at the time of incorporation in North Carolina, along with annual state and local taxes.

Expenditures

Money which may be used for any state activity—except for highway programs—comes from the general fund. This fund, supplemented by federal funds and special receipts, is used to pay recurring expenses for the administration of the state and its programs. It may also be used for such non-recurring purposes as construction and major repairs of state facilities.

An indication of the way state funds have been spent is the budget for fiscal year 1981, in which almost 40% of the budget was appropriated for the public schools—student services, teachers' salaries, programs for exceptional children and transportation. Another 18.3% of the total budget went for higher education and related programs. Highway fund expenditures for construction, maintenance and related expenses amounted to 15.3% of that total budget. Health, welfare and rehabilitation programs received the fourth largest chunk of state money.

Federal Funds

A large amount of money comes to North Carolina in the form of federal funds for specific programs. Although the dollars have increased, the average annual growth rate of federal funds has been decreasing rapidly in recent years, a trend that is expected to continue. Some 300 federal grants were included in the 1982-83 budget; 90% of the funds were concentrated in 18 programs. Most federal funds were to be received in that year by four departments: Human Resources (anticipating nearly half of all federal funds), Public Education, Transportation and Natural Resources and Community Development.

A large portion of federal funds received by state agencies is transferred to local governments, primarily for education, employment, social services and health programs.

CHAPTER VII.

RESPONSIBILITIES AND RIGHTS OF THE VOTER

As society becomes more complex and interdependent, so governmental institutions become larger and command a more pervasive role in the lives of citizens. This reality cannot be ignored. A democracy can be open and resilient only so long as the public controls governmental decisions. An absolute prerequisite to control is knowledge. Without guaranteed access by the public to governmental information and meetings of governmental bodies, no effort to decentralize decision-making or to otherwise increase public participation can succeed.

—Government in the Sunshine[1]

Rights of Access to Government

Citizens have a right to be informed about the government which is supported by their taxes. In 1971, the General Assembly enacted a "sunshine" or open meetings law to protect and promote this right. After the need for several rulings regarding interpretation, the General Assembly in 1979 revised the law providing for public notice of and

1. Ronald L. Plesser and Peter J. Petkas, *Government in the Sunshine: Open Records/Open Meetings, Emphasis: North Carolina*, (Atlanta: Southern Regional Council, 1975), pp. 8-9.

public access to all governmental meetings, with several exceptions. Major exceptions include the committees and subcommittees of the General Assembly, the Council of State, the Advisory Budget Commission, the Legislative Research Commission and the Judicial Standards Commission. (The rules of both the House and Senate call for open committee meetings, however, except when it is necessary to keep order or deemed "in the best interest of the state."[2]) The law (G.S. 143-318.9) also lists 18 subjects for which an executive session of an otherwise public meeting may be called.

Citizens may speak at most legislative committee hearings and even request that a public hearing be held on proposed legislation. Citizens are encouraged to attend and speak on specific matters at public hearings scheduled by executive department agencies and commissions. The Administrative Procedures Act of 1974 (G.S. 150A-1 *et. seq.*) provides for public comment, written or oral, before public agencies adopt, amend or repeal their rules and regulations.

For complete information about meetings of governmental bodies and access to public records, a citizen should contact appropriate officials or offices. (See Appendix A for addresses and telephone numbers.)

Political Parties

Political parties play a major role in government in that they recruit or support candidates who usually endorse the "platform" or objectives of the people who make up the party organization. Citizens have a responsibility to become involved in political activity at the party level if they wish to have a greater voice in candidate selection.

A political party is organized by means of precinct, county, congressional district, state and national committees. The rules for organization of each party are formulated by executive committees, with policies and platforms decided in conventions on the various levels. Rules of the different parties vary.

2. *North Carolina General Assembly, Senate Rules-Directory* and *House Rules-Directory*, (Raleigh: General Assembly, 1981), Senate Rule 36 and House Rule 28(b).

Political parties must be officially recognized by the State Board of Elections in order for citizens to register as a member and for candidates to be placed on any ballot. The General Assembly has defined a political party as any group of voters that polled at least ten percent of the total vote cast for its candidate for governor or for presidential electors. To gain official recognition for a new party, a group must present to the State Board of Elections a petition signed by 5,000 qualified and registered voters. The petition must be signed by at least 200 registered voters from each of four congressional districts.

State campaign financing laws state that officially recognized political parties in North Carolina may receive general fund money. A taxpayer may designate a political party to receive a one dollar contribution from his or her North Carolina income tax payment. If the taxpayer wishes to make a contribution but not to designate a party, distribution to the parties is made proportionally according to statewide voter registration. Regulations dealing with contributions to and expenditures for political campaigns apply to all candidates for elective office in county, municipal or district government as well as for state offices.

Independent Candidates

Independent candidates may seek office in a general election by filing petitions with the appropriate Board of Elections (G.S. 163-122). Petition signatures must equal two percent of the total number of registered voters in the state for a statewide office, five percent of the total number of registered voters in a district for a Congressional, House, N.C. Senate or other district-wide seat, ten percent of the registered voters in a county for a county office and fifteen percent of the registered voters in a municipality for a city office.

State Board of Elections

The State Board of Elections was established as an independent agency by the 1974 General Assembly which transferred it from the jurisdiction of the Department of State. A full-time position since 1926, the director has responsibility for the administration of all laws relating to elections. Enforcement of campaign finance laws is the responsibility of the State Board of Elections and the attorney general.

The Board of Elections is made up of five members who are appointed by the governor for terms of four years. They must be registered voters, and no more than three may be from the same political party.

Voting—a Right and a Responsibility

A North Carolina citizen takes a direct part in statewide lawmaking only when voting on proposed constitutional amendments or statewide bond issues. In all other elections, he or she votes to delegate this citizen power to a chosen representative. In order to use this power, the citizen must accept responsibility for registering to vote and then casting a ballot in every election.

Voting rights are protected by the Constitutions of the United States and the state of North Carolina. Sections 9 and 10 of Article I of the N.C. Constitution state that elections shall be held often and that they shall be free. There are no property qualifications, poll taxes or literacy tests in the election process. The procedures of elections are established by laws passed by the General Assembly.

Facts for Voters

Qualifications for Registration

1. Every citizen of the United States, either native-born or naturalized, may register to vote.

2. A person who is 18 years of age or who will be 18 by the next general election may register to vote.

3. Any individual who has been a resident of the state and precinct for 30 days by the

date of the next election may register to vote.

4. A person who has been convicted of a felony (a crime punishable by imprisonment) is eligible to register and vote when rights of citizenship have been restored.

When, Where and How to Register

1. Eligible voters may register year-round except during the 21 business days prior to an election. Registration for future elections may be made during that 21-day period. Registration may be made on the day of election by persons whose qualifications to vote mature at some time between the 21-day deadline and election day, such as persons becoming naturalized citizens or having rights of citizenship restored. Persons who become 18 years old or who meet the prescribed residence requirements after the 21-day deadline are not eligible to register on election day since they could have registered before the deadline in anticipation of meeting the requirements.

2. The County Board of Elections office is the primary place to register, but many counties have taken advantage of the law that allows permanent registration sites in public libraries and designated banks. Election supervisors may schedule special registration opportunities at shopping centers, park festivals, churches and other locations or may appoint registration commissioners to conduct voter registration at designated locations.

3. The State Board of Elections has ruled that registration to vote may be made at the

    homes of precinct registrars or judges of election, by appointment.

4. Identification will be required at the time of registration, such as a driver's license or birth certificate.

5. Members of the Armed Forces, their spouses, certain veterans and civilians with the Armed Forces or Peace Corps may register and vote by mail.

Political Party Affiliation

At the time of registration, eligible voters are asked to declare political party affiliation. A person registering may affiliate with one of the officially recognized political parties or register as an unaffiliated voter. (Officially recognized parties for the 1982 elections were Democratic, Libertarian, Republican and Socialist Workers Party.)

To vote in a political party's primary election, a person must be registered as affiliated with that party. During a partisan primary election, unaffiliated voters may vote only on the non-partisan candidates, referenda or bond issues. A voter may change political party affiliation or change from unaffiliated to political party affiliation any time the registration books are open. Changes may not be made on the day of primary elections.

Need for Reregistration

A voter need not reregister for each election, unless:

1. The voter has not voted in at least one of the last two presidential elections or any election in between and his or her name has been removed from the registration files.

2. The voter moves from one county or state to another.

3. The voter wishes to change party affiliation.

A voter who moves from one precinct to another within the county need not reregister but must file a written report, in person or by mail, with the county Board of Elections before the registration deadline. A voter who changes his or her name must report the change to the County Board of Elections before the registration deadline. However, if the voter fails to meet the deadline, the name change may be reported to the precinct registrar on election day, and, if otherwise qualified, the person may vote.

Voting on Election Day

Voters are assigned a precinct voting place and will be notified of its location at the time of registration or by mail prior to the first election. The polls are open from 6:30 a.m. until 7:30 p.m. every election day.

Upon entering the voting place, a voter is asked to state name and address (and party if it is a primary election) to an election official. If properly registered, the voter is then given an authorization to vote by machine or to complete the ballot form. Voting methods in North Carolina include traditional paper ballots, lever voting machines and cards which are punched or marked.

Whether voting on machines or using other ballot forms, voters are entitled to cast their votes in secret. Assistance cannot be given to a voter unless requested by the voter. Any voter—disabled, illiterate, or not—is allowed, upon request, to have a "near relative" assist in the voting booth.[3] A physically disabled voter or an illiterate voter may ask for help from a "near relative," any other voter at the precinct who has not aided anyone else, or an election official. A blind person is entitled to help from any person of his or her choice.

If an aged or physically disabled voter is unable to enter the voting place, that person is allowed to vote either in a vehicle

---

3. A "near relative" legally is a spouse, parent, child, sister, brother, grandparent, grandchild or legal guardian.

or near the voting place (curbside voting) between 7 a.m. and 6 p.m.

The Board of Elections, election officials at the polling places or the local League of Women Voters can answer questions about the procedures of registering and voting.

Absentee Voting

Absentee ballots may be requested from the County Board of Elections by registered voters who expect to be out of the county for the whole time the polls are open or by those unable to go to the polls because of illness or physical disability. The request may be made in person, by mail or by a "near relative" or legal guardian. Citizens who live overseas may vote absentee in the state in which they last resided.

Absentee voting is not allowed in fire district elections.

Application for absentee balloting must be made by 5 p.m. on the Thursday preceding an election. If a voter becomes ill or disabled after that, the voter or a "near relative" must make written application for an absentee ballot by noon on the day before an election. The application must be signed by the voter or the relative, a witness and the attending physician.

Absentee ballots, if approved, are delivered to the voter by mail or in person. Ballots must be marked in the presence of an officer authorized to administer oaths (a notary public). Ballots must be returned to the County Board of Elections by 5 p.m. the day before an election.

One-stop absentee voting is available the business day following the close of registration and ends at 5 p.m. on the Thursday before the election. In one-stop absentee voting, application for an absentee ballot and voting are accomplished at the same time.

Elections

National, state and county elections are held in even-numbered years. Municipal elections are held in odd-numbered years. School board elections vary from one district to another.

RESPONSIBILITIES AND RIGHTS OF THE VOTER

North Carolina voters elect all state-level officials every presidential election year (years divisible by four). Members of the U.S. House of Representatives and the General Assembly are elected every two years.

One U.S. senator representing North Carolina will be elected in 1984 and every six years thereafter. The other senator will be elected in 1986 and every six years thereafter.

Primary elections are held to nominate candidates for offices to be voted on in the general election. The presidential preference, county and state primary elections are held the Tuesday after the first Monday in May.

Cities with partisan elections hold their primaries on the sixth Tuesday before the general election. A second primary, if necessary, is held on the third Tuesday before the general election. Cities with nonpartisan primaries hold the primary on the fourth Tuesday before the general election.[4]

General elections are held the Tuesday after the first Monday in November. Cities that have a nonpartisan election and a run-off hold the election on the fourth Tuesday before the general election day and the run-off, if necessary, on general election day.[5]

Special elections may be called by the city, county, state or special district for purposes of submitting proposals to the voters such as bond issues or liquor referenda. Special elections may be held at the same time as primary or general elections or at some other time.

Responsive Government

The government of North Carolina is one in which elected officials are expected to be responsive to their constituents, even though they cannot agree with each individual at all times. Every citizen has the right to contact representatives in government in person, by telephone or in writing in order to explain and urge support of specific ideas and opinions. In this way, the citizen exercises power in a representative democracy.

4. H. Rutherford Turnbull, III., *The Precinct Manual/1980*, (Chapel Hill: Institute of Government, 1980), p. 9.
5. *Ibid.*

Appendix A

COMMUNICATING WITH GOVERNMENT

Citizens can be effective when they express an informed opinion to the appropriate officials at the right time.

WRITE A LETTER:
   Make your letter legible; handwritten letters are
      preferable.
   Use your own words and your own stationery.
   Give your address and sign your name legibly.
   Speak to only one topic–give number of bill if possible.
   Be sure of your facts.
   Be brief and to the point.
   State your stand and your reasons.
   Be courteous and reasonable.
   Ask your questions in a way that requires a personal
      answer.
   Time your letter to coincide with a key decision-making
      point.
   Write to praise as well as to criticize.

SEND A MAILGRAM OR TELEGRAM:
   Use a Public Service Message form for "next day" delivery.
   This is most effective when vote or decision is imminent.

TELEPHONE:
   Effective because you get an answer immediately.
   Follow your call with a letter summarizing your point of
      view.

Map of Downtown State Government Complex

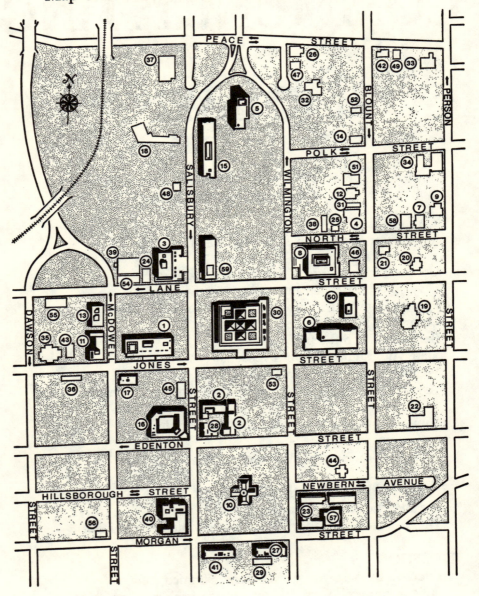

Legend

1. Administration Building
   116 W Jones Street
2. Agriculture Building & Annex
   1 W Edenton Street
3. Albemarle Building
   325 N Salisbury Street
4. Andrew Duncan House
   407 N Blount Street
5. Archdale Building
   512 S Salisbury Street
6. Archives-Library Building
   109 E Jones Street
7. Ashley House
   219 E North Street
8. Bath Building
   306 N Wilmington Street
9. Cambridge House
   407 N Person Street
10. Capitol
    Capitol Square
11. Caswell Building
    200 W Jones Street
12. Coble-Helms House
    417 N Blount Street
13. Cooper Memorial Health Building
    225 N McDowell Street
14. Cowper House
    501 N Blount Street
15. Dobbs Building
    430 N Salisbury Street
16. Education Building
    114 W Edenton Street
17. Elks Building
    121 W Jones Street
18. General Services Building
    431 N Salisbury Street
19. Governor's Executive Mansion
    200 N Blount Street
20. Handy House
    215 E Lane Street
21. Hawkins-Hartness House
    310 N Blount Street
22. Heart of Raleigh Motel
    227 E. Edenton Street
23. Highway Building
    Corner of Wilmington St
    & New Bern Ave
24. Howard Building
    112 Lane Street
25. Howell House
    111 E North Street
26. Jordon House
    532 N Wilmington Street

27. Justice Building
    Corner of Fayetteville
    & Morgan Streets
28. Labor Building
    4 W Edenton Street
29. Law Building
    107 Fayetteville Street Mall
30. Legislative Building
    Jones Street
31. McGee House
    411 N Blount Street
32. Merrimon-Wynne House
    526 N Wilmington Street
33. Motor Pool Annex
    220 E Peace Street
35. Old Health Building
    215 W Jones Street
36. Old YWCA Building
    217 W Jones Street
37. Personnel Development Center
    101 W Peace Street
38. Phillips Building
    109 E North Street
39. Printing Office, State Government
    300 N McDowell Street
40. Revenue Building
    2 S Salisbury Street
41. Ruffin Building
    1 W Morgan Street
42. Russ-Edwards House
    540 N Blount Street
43. Shore Building
    214 W Jones Street
44. State Employees Credit Union
    119 N Salisbury Street
46. Visitor Center
    301 N Blount Street
47. Watson House
    530 N Wilmington Street
48. Womack Building
    417 N Salisbury Street
49. Worth House
    210 E Peace Street
50. 215 N Blount Street
51. 421 N Blount Street
52. 515 N Blount Street
53. 10 E Jones Street
54. 120 W Lane Street
55. 215 W Lane Street
56. 10 S McDowell Street
57. 107 E Morgan Street
58. 217 North Street
59. 300 N Salisbury Street

NORTH CAROLINA: OUR STATE GOVERNMENT

ADDRESSING STATE OFFICIALS:

The Honorable —————
Governor of North Carolina
Raleigh, North Carolina 27611

Dear Governor —————:

The Honorable —————
House of Representatives
Raleigh, North Carolina 27611

Dear Representative—————:

The Honorable—————
The Senate
Raleigh, North Carolina 27611

Dear Senator—————:

ADDRESSES AND TELEPHONE NUMBERS OF MAJOR STATE OFFICES

State government telephone numbers in Raleigh have 733 as the prefix. The area code is 919.

Secretary of Administration, Administration Building, 116 W. Jones St., Raleigh 27611	7232
Administrative Office of the Courts, Justice Building, Fayetteville & Morgan Sts., Raleigh 27611	7107
Commissioner of Agriculture, Agriculture Building, 1 W. Edenton St., Raleigh 27611	7125
Attorney General, Justice Building, Fayetteville & Morgan Sts., Raleigh 27611	3377
State Auditor, Legislative Office Building, 300 N. Salisbury St., Raleigh 27611	3217
Secretary of Commerce, Dobbs Building, 430 N. Salisbury St., Raleigh 27611	4962
Secretary of Correction, 840 W. Morgan St., Raleigh 27603	4926

COMMUNICATING WITH GOVERNMENT

Council on the Status of Women, 526 N.
    Wilmington St., Raleigh 27604   2455

Secretary of Crime Control and Public Safety,
    Archdale Building, 512 N. Salisbury St.,
    Raleigh 27611   2126

Secretary of Cultural Resources, Archives-Library
    Building, 109 E. Jones St., Raleigh 27611   4867

State Board of Elections, 5 W. Hargett St.,
    Raleigh 27611   7218

Office of the Governor, State Capitol Building,
    Capitol Square, Raleigh 27611   5811

Governor's Advocacy Council for Children and
    Youth, 112 W. Lane St., Raleigh 27611   6880

Governor's Advocacy Council for Persons with
    Disabilities, 112 W. Lane St., Raleigh 27611 3111

Secretary of Human Resources, Albemarle
    Building, 325 N. Salisbury St., Raleigh 27611 4534

Commissioner of Insurance, Dobbs Building,
    431 N. Salisbury St., Raleigh 27611   7343

Commissioner of Labor, Labor Building, 4 W.
    Edenton St., Raleigh 27611   7166

Legislative Building Receptionist, Legislative
    Building, Jones St., Raleigh 27611   3813

Legislative Switchboard (during sessions)   4111

Lieutenant Governor, Room 2017, Legislative
    Office Building, 300 N. Salisbury St.,
    Raleigh 27611   7351

Secretary of Natural Resources and Community
    Development, Archdale Building, 512 N.
    Salisbury St., Raleigh 27611   4984

Department of Public Education, Superintendent
    of Public Instruction, Education Building,
    114 W. Edenton St., Raleigh 27611   3813

Secretary of Revenue, Revenue Building, 2 S.
    Salisbury St., Raleigh 27611   7211

Secretary of State, State Capitol Building, Capitol
    Square, Raleigh 27611   3433

Secretary of Transportation, Highway Building,
    1 S. Wilmington St., Raleigh 27611   2520

State Treasurer, Albemarle Building, 325 N.
Salisbury St., Raleigh 27611   3951

TOLL-FREE TELEPHONE NUMBERS

Care-Line, Information and Referral Center, Dept. of Human Resources	800-662-7030
Energy Hotline, Department of Commerce	800-662-7131
Governor's Office of Citizen Affairs	800-662-7952
Insurance Department (Consumer Affairs)	800-662-7777
Library for the Blind	800-662-7726
Market Report, Department of Agriculture	800-662-7573
Medicaid Eligibility Verification (for providers only)	800-662-7547
N.C. State Library	800-662-7644
Office of Local Government/Advocacy	800-662-7200
Teletip, Agricultural Extension Service	800-662-7301

INDEPENDENT STATE BOARDS AND COMMISSIONS

Advisory Budget Commission
North Carolina Alcoholism Research Authority
Legislative Commission on Children with Special Needs
North Carolina Courts Commission
State Education Association Authority, Board of Directors
Southeastern Interstate Forest Fire Protection Compact Advisory Committee
Judicial Council
Judicial Standards Commission
Southern Growth Policies Board
Southern Interstate Nuclear Board
Board of Control for Southern Regional Education
Tax Study Commission
The Central Orphanage of North Carolina Board of Directors
State Board of Elections
North Carolina Board of Ethics
North Carolina Fisheries Association, Board of Directors
Committee on Inaugural Ceremonies
Judicial Nominating Committee for Superior Court Judges
USS Monitor Research Council

If you wish to write to any of these groups, address them as follows:

(Name of board)
State of North Carolina
Raleigh, North Carolina 27611

LICENSING BOARDS

North Carolina Board of Architecture
North Carolina Auctioneers Commission
State Board of Barbers Examiners
State Board of Certified Public Accountants
Child Day Care Licensing Board
North Carolina Hearing Aid Dealers and
    Fitters Board
North Carolina Licensing Board for
    Landscape Architects
North Carolina Landscape Contractors'
    Registration Board
North Carolina Board of Nursing
North Carolina State Board of Examiners for
    Nursing Home Administrators
North Carolina State Board of Opticians
North Carolina State Board of Examiners in
    Optometry
State Board of Osteopathic Examiners and
    Registration
State Board of Pharmacy
North Carolina State Examining Committee
    of Physical Therapy
State Board of Examiners of Plumbing and
    Heating Contractors
North Carolina State Board of Examiners of
    Practicing Psychologists
Private Protective Services Board
North Carolina Real Estate Licensing Board
State Board of Refrigeration Examiners
State Board of Registration for Professiona'
    Engineers and Land Surveyors

State Board of Sanitarian Examiners
North Carolina Veterinary Medical Board
State Board of Chiropractic Examiners
State Licensing Board for Contractors
State Board of Cosmetic Art Examiners
State Board of Examiners of Electrical
    Contractors
State Board of Registration of Foresters
State Board of Examiners of Electrical
    Contractors
North Carolina Board of Mortuary Science
North Carolina Manufactured Housing Board

BIBLIOGRAPHY

Administrative Office of the Courts, *North Carolina Courts, 1979-80, Annual Report* (Raleigh: Administrative Office of the Courts, January, 1981).

Thad L. Beyle, "How Powerful is the North Carolina Governor?" *N.C. Insight*, Vol. 4, No. 4 (December, 1981).

John L. Cheney, Jr. (Editor), *North Carolina Manual* (Raleigh: Office of the Secretary of State, 1979).

John L. Cheney, Jr., *North Carolina Government—1585-1974: A Narrative and Statistical History* (Raleigh: Office of the Secretary of State, 1975).

James W. Clay, Douglas M. Orr, Jr., and Alfred W. Stuart, *North Carolina Atlas* (Chapel Hill: The University of North Carolina Press, 1975).

Albert Coates, *Talks to Students and Teachers: The Structure and Workings of Government in the Cities and the Counties and the State of North Carolina* (Chapel Hill: Creative Printers, 1971).

Albert Coates, *The Public Schools and the Eighteen-Year-Old Voters* (Chapel Hill: The University of North Carolina Press, 1975).

Albert Coates, *Bridging the Gap Between Government in Books and Government in Action* (Chapel Hill: the University of North Carolina Press, 1975).

Michael Crowell and Milton S. Heath, Jr., *The General Assembly of North Carolina: A Handbook for Legislators* (fourth edition), (Chapel Hill: Institute of Government, 1981).

Wilma R. Davidson (Editor), *Annual Directory of North Carolina Organizations* (Charlotte: North Carolina Council of Women's Organizations, Inc., 1976).

Stephen N. Dennis, *Index to Computer Print Out of Governor's Appointment Powers* (Chapel Hill: Institute of Government, 1975).

"Factors Favorable to Industry in North Carolina," (Raleigh: N.C. Department of Commerce, Industrial Development Division, undated).

Joseph S. Ferrell (Editor), *County Government in North Carolina* (Chapel Hill: Institute of Government, 1975).

Edwin Gill, *Biennial Report of the Treasurer of North Carolina* (Raleigh: State of North Carolina, 1975).

Senator John T. Henley, *State Government Reorganization in North Carolina* (Raleigh: State of North Carolina, 1970).

Institute of Government, *Chart of the Administrative Organization of North Carolina State Government* (Chapel Hill: Institute of Government, August 1, 1971).

Institute of Government, *Chart of the Interim Effects of Reorganization Upon the Administrative Organization of North Carolina State Government* (Chapel Hill: Institute of Government, August 1, 1972).

Institute of Government, *North Carolina Legal Aspects of Doing Business* (Raleigh: N.C. Department of Natural and Economic Resources, 1974).

Richard H. Leach, "Book Tells Tarheels About State," *Durham Morning Herald*, Jan. 16, 1977.

League of Women Voters of North Carolina, *ABC's of Voting and Registration* (Durham: League of Women Voters of North Carolina, 1980.).

League of Women Voters of North Carolina (Sylvia Ruby, Editor), *It's Your State—North Carolina* (Durham: League of Women Voters of North Carolina, 1969).

League of Women Voters of North Carolina (Wilma R. Davidson, Editor), *North Carolina: Our State Government* (Durham: League of Women Voters of North Carolina, 1976).

League of Women Voters of Missouri, *Missouri Voters' Handbook* (St. Louis: League of Women Voters of Missouri, 1975).

League of Women Voters of Virginia, *Your Virginia State Government* (Vienna, Virginia: League of Women Voters of Virginia, 1975).

League of Women Voters of Wisconsin, *Know Your State Wisconsin* (Madison: League of Women Voters of Wisconsin, 1974).

Hugh T. Lefler and Albert R. Newsome, *North Carolina: The*

BIBLIOGRAPHY

History of a Southern State (3rd Ed.) (Chapel Hill: UNC Press, 1973).

Hugh T. Lefler and William S. Powell, *Colonial North Carolina* (New York: Charles Scribner's Sons, 1973).

Memory F. Mitchell (Editor), *Addresses and Public Papers of Robert W. Scott, 1969-1973* (Raleigh: Division of Archives and History, Department of Cultural Resources, 1974).

North Carolina Citizens Association, *North Carolina* (14th Annual Transportation Issue), (Raleigh: North Carolina Citizens Association, July, 1975).

North Carolina Constitution (as of July 1, 1980), issued by Thad Eure, Secretary of State.

North Carolina Department of Correction, *Probation and Parole: Invisible Bars* (Raleigh: Department of Correction, undated).

North Carolina Department of Labor with U.S. Bureau of Labor Statistics, *Trends in Employment, Hours, and Earnings* (Raleigh: N.C. Department of Labor, January, 1976).

North Carolina Department of Natural and Economic Resources, *North Carolina Historyland* (Raleigh: Department of Natural and Economic Resources, Travel and Promotion Division, undated).

North Carolina Department of Natural and Economic Resources, *North Carolina State and Local Taxes* (Raleigh: Department of Natural and Economic Resources, 1975).

North Carolina General Assembly, *Senate Rules-Directory* (Raleigh: North Carolina General Assembly, 1981).

North Carolina General Assembly, *House Rules-Directory* (Raleigh: North Carolina General Assembly, 1981).

North Carolina State Data Center, Vol. 3, No. 2 (Raleigh: Office of State Budget and Management, April, 1981).

North Carolina: Tax Guide 1981 (Raleigh: Office of State Budget and Management, 1981).

Ronald L. Plesser and Peter J. Petkas, *Government in the Sunshine: Open Records/Open Meetings, Emphasis: North Carolina* (Atlanta: Southern Regional Council, 1975).

William S. Powell, *Ye County of Albemarle* (Raleigh: North Carolina Department of Archives and History, 1958).

John L. Sanders, *Amendments to the Constitution of North Carolina 1776-1974* (Chapel Hill: Institute of Government, 1975).

Barbara Smith (Editor), *Assembly Assignment* (Durham: League of Women Voters of North Carolina, 1975).

State of North Carolina, *The General Assembly of North Carolina* (Raleigh: State of North Carolina, undated pamphlet).

State of North Carolina, *Summary of the Recommended State Budget, 1981-83 Biennium* (Raleigh: Office of State Budget and Management, 1981).

H. Rutherford Turnbull III, *The Precinct Manual/1980, North Carolina Election Law and Procedure for Precinct Officials* (Chapel Hill: Institute of Government, 1980).

INDEX